CHRISTIANITY AND THE WORLD ORDER

THE B.B.C. REITH LECTURES, 1978

Christianity and the World Order

EDWARD NORMAN

Dean of Peterhouse, Cambridge

Oxford New York Toronto Melbourne
OXFORD UNIVERSITY PRESS
1979

Oxford University Press, Walton Street, Oxford OX2 6DP

Oxford London Glasgow
New York Toronto Melbourne Wellington
Kuala Lumpur Singapore Jakarta Hong Kong Tokyo
Denhi Bombay Calcutta Madras Karachi
Ibadan Nairobi Dar Es Salaam Cape Town

© *E.R. Norman 1979*

British Library Cataloguing in Publication Data
Norman, Edward Robert
  Christianity and the world order. — (Reith lectures; 1978).
  1. Christianity and politics
  I. Title   II. Series
  261.7   BR115.P7   78—40857
  ISBN 0 19 215510 5
  ISBN 0 19 283019 8   Pbk

Typeset by Oxford Publishing Services, Oxford.
Printed in Great Britain by
Billing & Sons Ltd., Guildford and Worcester.

Contents

1. The political Christ   1

2. Ministers of change   15

3. A new Commandment: Human Rights   29

4. The imperialism of political religion   43

5. Not peace, but a sword   57

6. 'The indwelling Christ'   72

   Notes   86

   Index   101

1 | *The political Christ*

Towards the end of 1975, an impressive assortment of Christians gathered in Nairobi for the Fifth Assembly of the World Council of Churches. Some in the splendours of ethnic dress, and some others in the scarcely less exotic costumes of the various denominations, their procession at the opening ceremony extended backwards from the Jomo Kenyatta Conference Centre until it curled around the huge statue of Kenyatta himself in the forecourt some distance away. It was, altogether, a visible sign of the shifting balance in the numerical centre of Christianity, away from the countries of Europe and North America, and towards the nations of the developing world. The theme of the gathering, itself expressing the 'Third World' flavour of contemporary international Christianity, was *Jesus Christ Frees and Unites*. The main exposition came in a speech from Dr. Robert McAfee Brown, Professor of World Christianity at Union Theological Seminary in New York City. Confessing that as a white, male, bourgeois American, he embodied what he called 'racism, sexism, classism and imperialism', and more than adequately apologizing for the sins in which this involved him, he lapsed into Spanish, apparently in an attempt to avoid, as he put it, the 'linguistic imperialism' of the English tongue. Most of those present reached for their translation headsets.[1] It was a symbolic moment. What they heard was later described, in the official Church of England report, as 'a major theological address.'[2] Dr McAfee Brown spoke of Jesus as 'Liberator', concerned with 'social, political and economic liberation.' And after dwelling at some length upon the identification of Christianity with the demands of 'oppressed peoples', as he put it, he went on to say: 'you may feel that I have not made Jesus political enough, and that I am too conditioned by bourgeois categories to understand the full thrust of liberation.'[3] It was, in the circumstances, a modest disclaimer.

This incident, in itself typical enough, discloses the most remarkable of all the changes that have occurred within Christianity during the last twenty years. For both individual Christian leaders, and the churches collectively, have undergone a process known to social scientists and historians as *politicization*. The nature of this change, and its effects, is the theme of these lectures. Politicization does not mean mere political activity — indeed some politicized Christians, like those in England, are notable for a very low level of participation in actual political organization. By the politicization of religion is meant the internal transformation of the faith itself, so that it comes to be defined in terms of political values — it becomes essentially concerned with social morality rather than with the ethereal qualities of immortality. Christianity today is, in this sense, being reinterpreted as a scheme of social and political action, dependent, it is true, upon supernatural authority for its ultimate claims to attention, but rendered in categories that are derived from the political theories and practices of contemporary society. There are several versions of this tendency, and there are varying degrees of coherence in the extent to which it is accomplished; but all start from a rejection of preceding Christian attitudes, from a belief that Christians have in the past been too concerned with spirituality. Religious engagement with the world was seen to be an affair of charitable palliatives. In its place, contemporary Christians seek a corporate reaction to what are increasingly regarded as collective sins: racism, economic or cultural exploitation, class division, the denial of Human Rights, and so forth. This concept is itself a clue to what has happened. Christians are responding sympathetically to the creation of collectivist state structures, and to the secular moral assumptions which sustain their authority. The attitudes of Christians are, therefore, like those of society in general. Some of their present political consciousness is forced upon the Churches. The increasing politicization of *all* moral values in our society, and the extension of the social competence of government, have prompted the entry of the state into areas which were formerly the traditional preserve of the Churches — education, for example, and very many other aspects of social welfare. These incursions make it very difficult for the Church *not* to become politically involved, for politics has actually moved into its own sphere.

The present reinterpretation of Christianity goes deeper than these conditions oblige, however, and is, in reality, an expression of the politicization of the clergy themselves, both personally and as a class. They have allowed themselves — some eagerly, and many others unwittingly — to define their religious values according to the categories and references provided by the compulsive moralism of contemporary intellectual culture. This is not, of course, the way they see things themselves. They believe they are bringing a Christian critique to bear upon the great problems of the day; that they comprise an external body of ideals. But that is not actually the case, due to the progressive secularization of the values to which their own understanding of religion is made to correspond. Between a Christian knowledge of politics acquired in order to serve the interests of the Church as an institution, and the identification of the content of the faith with human attempts at social improvement, there is a fundamental difference. 'I regard politics as a necessary evil in the life of a priest', Cardinal József Mindszenty once said.[4] Today's Christianity, however, increasingly regards politics as a primary virtue. It is this development which makes the present association between Christianity and political values unlike past ones. The history of Europe since the conversion of Constantine is a history of Christian involvement with the political order. But in former experiences of Christian political action the distinction between the sacred and the secular, between Church and State, was much less clearly drawn than it now is, in the modern secular framework. Indeed the Church's past involvements with world order produced just as much a 'sacralizing' of politics as it did a politicization of the faith. Acting from within the structure, in which they occupied a position of confidence and privilege, the clergy did not, in general, adopt the characteristically politicized outlook which they do who operate from outside a system and seek its radical transformation. There is, then, a clear distinction between the involvement of religion with politics and the reinterpretation of religious values as political values — which is what occurs in the process of politicization, and is what is happening in the modern Church.

The Christian religion has lost the power, and also the confidence, to define the areas of public debate, even in moral questions. Instead, it follows the definitions made by others. Almost no one now looks to the Church for social teaching, though in the Third World religion still has a social role. Even the fears of impending global chaos or annihilation do not elicit religious responses, as once the intimations of cataclysm would have done. The contemporary debate about world resources, over-population, pollution, or nuclear catastrophe, is according to the analyses of secular thinkers — although the Churches tag along, offering a religious gloss to precisely the same ideas. No one listens, for religion is no longer regarded as a guarantor of stability.

It is important to ask whether Christian influence may be more decisive in those parts of the Third World in which the Church is strong, in Africa and South America especially. It is easy, from the perspective of western society, not to realize that this is, in fact, a great period of Christian expansion. There are an estimated 55,000 Christian conversions every day throughout the world[5] — a staggering figure by any standards, and the more so when it is set against the decay of the western churches. But there are imponderables about future developments. At present Christianity is closely associated with the buoyant movements for national identity and change in the developing world, but will its role be curtailed by the spread of western secularization? Will the extensive criticism of inherited western values — in which the Church takes a prominent part — have the effect of preparing the ground for the eventual success of Marxism in the Third World, especially now that Marxism seems so often to be the form in which the moral seriousness of the new educated classes express themselves? And will Marxist political societies necessarily result in the progressive decline of religious institutions? The developing world is characterized by sharply rising expectations as to what can be achieved by social change and political action — and, again, the Churches have thrown their influence onto the side of those who encourage this development. But these expectations are really out of all proportion to the opportunities of meeting them, and the long term consequences of that will surely involve the creation of monolithic controlled societies. Will the Churches survive within their own creation? And, despite appearances to the contrary, the ideas that inspire the political consciousness of the developing world's Christianity actually originate within the politicized Churches of the old world, where Christianity is in radical decay. Most Third World Christianity is spiritual rather than political, but everywhere church leadership tends to consist of westernized élites who superimpose the liberal and radical political idealism of the Christian thinking of the developed world upon the diffused religiosity round them. The result is an appearance of authenticity: their westernized political Christianity, as in the ideologies of African nationalism, is mistaken for the voice of the world's oppressed. I shall, in these lectures, illustrate this feature with analyses of the Christian thinking of Latin America and Southern Africa. In their death agonies, therefore, the western Churches are distributing the causes of their own sickness — the politicization of religion — to their healthy offspring in the developing world. Will it prove a fatal inheritance, or will the vibrant Churches of the Southern Hemisphere become, in the end, sufficiently inventive to produce their own antidotes? The spread of education is another crucial consideration. There is no doubt that in developed societies education has contributed to the decline of religious belief. But there is nothing determined about it. Everything depends upon the values the educators convey. In Victorian Britain popular education was promoted by a class which was soaked in religious moralism, and the result was the distribution of a reasonably uniform if diluted Christian culture. Modern educationalists are secular in outlook, but also committed moralists. So their endeavours spread secular morality. The outcome of mass education in the developing world is entirely dependent upon the presuppositions of those who carry it out. There is nothing in the enlightenment of the mind, as such, that leads to scepticism. Religious belief, like other ideals in the modern world, is sustained by élites. If Christianity is dropped from the agenda of the predominant élites it will in the course of time decline.

In the developed western nations the politicization of Christianity is already very advanced. It takes the form of identifying Christian teachings with the moral outlook and political ideals of liberalism. Christians themselves, of course, only believe that they are endorsing agreed moral truths -- providing a religious foundation for the higher principles which liberalism promotes. They see such concepts as democratic pluralism, equality, individualist Human Rights, the freedom to choose values, and so forth, as basic expressions of Christianity, the modern applications of the moral precepts of Christ. But to an external observer, or to non-liberals, their commitment to these principles looks like ordinary political preference. To Marxists, the fundamental principles of liberalism, together with their religious backing, are merely formalized expressions of class ideology. Criticisms of capitalism — which are now the staple matter of much Christian social commentary (but criticisms which leave the basis of the social system undisturbed) appear at best trivial, at worst hypocritical.[6] To those who are sceptical of all versions of Christian politics, including conservative ones — and this is my own position — the present identification of Christianity with western bourgeois liberalism seems an unnecessary consecration of a highly relative and unstable set of values, the more unsatisfactory because it is generally done unconsciously. Liberalism actually occupies a very narrow band in the possible spectrum of political theories. To regard it as the distillation of Christian wisdom, as the contemporary repository of a timeless faith, is, to say the least, a short-term view. But related by class and cultural preference to the educated élites whose endorsement of liberal values they so faithfully reproduce, the leaders of the western churches seem completely unaware of how partial their political vision actually is. It may well be, of course, that liberalism is perfectly acceptable for all kinds of political and moral reasons: my contention is simply that there are no distinctly *Christian* reasons for regarding its principles as more compatible with the teachings of Christ than other and rival political outlooks. Church leaders seem unaware of the problem.

Let me give an example. In November last year, during the press conference to announce a Church of England report on the closed shop in industry, the Bishop of Worcester described 'tolerant attitudes, flexibility, and compassion' as 'the Christian virtues which have got to be transfused into society'. It was, he added, 'the role of the Church to see that such principles were at work.'[7] Now 'tolerance', 'flexibility' and 'compassion' are not distinctively Christian virtues, though two of them are arguably classical pagan ones, nor does an examination of the history of Christianity suggest that the Church is the most suitable agency to secure their application. And anyway, whatever the pedigree of these concepts, the fact is that their real virtue is entirely dependent upon the ideas to which they are made to relate; and that is something which alters according to circumstance and the general prescriptions of the prevailing ideology. The Bishop's patronage of these selected qualities turns out to be sponsorship of the content of contemporary liberalism. Here is another example: at the Caxton Hall conference on religious education, in February 1978, the Archbishop of Canterbury asked, 'Do we want to indoctrinate children into our own beliefs?' He answered, 'God forbid.' There was, he said, a need instead to introduce children to a 'discussion' of religion.[8] What the Archbishop's words actually convey is approval of the contemporary liberal belief that society should consist of a balanced pluralism of moral opinion, and that people should be free to select their own values. This scheme of things is so frequently expressed, and so unquestioningly accepted within the western liberal intelligentsia, that its advocates are innocently unaware of just how politically partial it is. Some pretence is also involved, because liberals certainly believe in the indoctrination of their own liberalism. On such issues as race or educational equalitarianism western liberals are clearly not prepared to allow public debate to go undirected. No one who really believes in his values leaves their acceptance to chance, particularly when it comes to children. Marxists don't; nor should Christians — whose business is indoctrination if it is anything. And in practice Christians *are* found calling for the enforcement of ideas. But it is not religious ideas that the state is to propagate — for that is regarded by them as illiberal. It is the components of the contemporary liberal creed, the virtues of social democracy, that they wish to see enforced.

This year's Lambeth Conference, of the bishops of the Anglican Communion, was richly imbued with Christian endorsements of liberal idealism.[9] Beginning with the un-likely spectacle of the bishops processing into Canterbury Cathedral to the accompaniment of *The Groovers* steel band — apparently intended to evoke the spirit of the Third World — the tone of the Conference was set by two 'Special Lectures' delivered in the opening days. Both were full of moralistic criticism of western capitalism and of the present application of technology by the developed nations. Both were extremely partial, reducing highly technical information to simple dismissals of alternative viewpoints — treating the governments of the Western world, and the great weight of scientific and technical opinion, as if they were childishly ignorant of practical as well as moral considerations. The bishops were lyrical in their approval. The lecture by Barbara Ward (Lady Jackson) — which the Archbishop of Canterbury later described as 'wonderful' — vilified 'colonialism', referred approvingly to China's economic priorities, and contended for 'small scale' technology, in a sort of updated arts-and-crafts vision. The world's energy problem was to be met with solar panels — which had the additional advantage, according to Barbara Ward, of favouring the under-developed countries, because that is where the sunshine is. The second lecturer was Professor Charles Elliott, an adviser for some years to President Kaunda of Zambia. Present civilization was 'rotten', he said. 'Prophetic action' was needed, to end what he called 'the sin in the structures' of society. Technology had to be 'socially useful' to justify itself: he condemned the development of *Concorde.* To the assembled prelates it seemed as if the voice of truth was calling them to grapple with the real problems of the secular world. It was left to an Orthodox Archbishop, the Metropolitan Anthony, to remind them, in the second of his devotional addresses, that 'what we call *secular* would in the past have been called *pagan.'*

It was the conflation of Christian morality and Humanist ethics, made by so many theologians and Church leaders during the 1960's, that decisively secularized important aspects of Christianity, though other causes had been at work before that. This contributed also to its politicization. For Humanists seek to add to the competence of the political sphere by incorporating their moral beliefs about social welfare, and so on, into law. They demonstrate the modern tendency to regard all values as political values. Even in areas where their ideals ostensibly require *less* state activity, as in the Humanist call for sexual conduct to be freed from legislative interference — a call, incidentally, generally welcomed by Christian leaders on liberal grounds — even in such areas, the experience of organization and agitation for reform is itself profoundly politicizing in its effects. The view of human nature expressed by Humanism is in direct contradiction to received religious attitudes, as Humanists themselves have always insisted. The 1960's crisis of values within the western intelligentsia ought to have elicited a clear polarization

between religious and secular attitudes on such fundamental matters as the doctrine of man. In practice this did
not happen, and at least part of the explanation is to be
found in the willingness of Christian thinkers to adopt the
same moral and intellectual outlook as the Humanists.
Humanists, for their part, adopted none of the premises of
Christianity. But their view of man as morally autonomous
and capable of progressive development, and the calculated
hedonism of Humanist ethics, penetrated far into Christian
attitudes during the 1960's, so that eventually even the
most broad and liberal of the bishops started describing
themselves as 'Christian Humanists' — and not, I should
add, in the tradition of Erasmus, but in deference to the
secular luminaries of the time. What Ivan Illich called a
'radical secularization' of the whole structure of institutional Christianity[10] was regarded by some as a necessary
consequence of the Christian discovery of the ideals inherent in contemporary moral seriousness. Some others
were less impressed. Speaking in the cathedral of Bogotá,
during his visit to Colombia in 1968, the late Pope Paul
said: 'The gaps left in our schools of philosophy by this
loss of confidence in the great masters of Christian thought,
has all too often been filled by a superficial and almost ser-
vile acceptance of the currently fashionable philosophies.'[11]
The evaporation of any sense that religious tradition conveys a unique understanding of human life has been one of
the most decisive changes in modern Christian experience.
Instead of modifying or rejecting secular culture, the most
influential of Christian thinkers have adopted it. The
whole emphasis of contemporary Christianity eschews
traditional doctrinal priorities, and is about applications.
The Church is increasingly preoccupied with the pursuit of
a more just society, and with the material problems of
humanity. Secular programmes for human improvement
seem more important, as practical if unconscious ex-

pressions of God's love, than does the cultivation of correct religious belief. Churchmen are, as it happens, rather selective in this, preferring to see the divine energy revealed in régimes that are not right-wing. Thus China, whose denial of the most basic Human Rights ought to attract the condemnation of those Christians whose liberalism is the most developed, is in practice often treated to positively fulsome praise. Here is an account of the 'China Study Presentation' made to the Spring Assembly of the British Council of Churches:

'After slides had been shown' — according to the report — 'the Projects Officer (the Reverend Bob Whyte) spoke of China's efforts to produce a modern economy based on social justice. Miss Betty Bar, daughter of a one-time Shanghai missionary, spoke of the new sense of community in China now, the sense of pride and purpose and of the small Christian groups who function mainly without buildings, clergy or ritual. The Reverend (Miss) Lee Ching Chee (of Hong Kong) contrasted the many Churches in Hong Kong with the lack of them in China: she asked whether the people of Hong Kong were any more Christian than those of China. The Reverend Dr. John Fleming underlined this when he asserted that God still lives in China today, not because there are Christians there, but because He is at work there, confronting us with what He is doing through non-Christians, through science, through political leaders.'[12]

This type of assessment, like the accompanying readiness to identify with the social objectives of a rival ideology, indicates a real loss of confidence in the traditional claims of Christianity. It is a further acceptance of material tests as the criteria for moral worth. Christianity has an extraordinary propensity to regard its own replacements with benign approval.

This is not to say that the actual social and political ideals adopted by Christians are in themselves untrue, or are not in correspondence with a legitimate understanding of the faith. It is, however, to suggest that they are far too relative to be regarded as central in the definition of

Christianity itself. And it is certainly to look to the practical consequences: at what will happen to Christianity as its content is drained away into the great pool of secular idealism. It is to ask whether Christianity will not identify itself so closely with secular ideas that its fate will be inseparable from theirs.

These lectures will not be greatly concerned with the technical arguments to be found in the theological reinterpretations which are required to represent Christianity as a scheme of secular redemption. They will not primarily be an examination of what are called 'Political Theology', 'Liberation Theology' and 'Black Theology': systematic explanations of politicized religious values. I shall be concerned much more with the immediate motivations of Christian involvement with political issues. Since the exponents of Political Theology themselves declare that their intentions are activist rather than theoretical, they would perhaps agree that this is a reasonable procedure. I hope to isolate the political ideas used both consciously and unconsciously by contemporary Christians, to identify them, and to set them in the general context of political thinking and practice in the modern world. In the largest perspective, I shall see the politicization of Christianity as a symptom of its decay as an authentic religion. It is losing sight of its own rootedness in a spiritual tradition; its mind is progressively secularized; its expectations are prompted by worldly changes; and its moral idealism has forfeited transcendence. The prospects are not happy ones. The present decline of Christianity in the developed world, furthermore, is not the consequence of successful assault by its enemies. It is due to the surrender of its unique claims to an understanding of the nature of men made by its own leaders. As Bryan Wilson, the Oxford sociologist, has observed, the Churches have responded to secularization by the process of 'voluntary destructuration.'[13] They have given up their own forms and procedures in order to accommodate the new social attitudes. Fortunately, we may remember that truth does not cease because people give up believing it. In fact the decline of Christianity in the developed countries actually confirms the view of human nature which the Church itself once taught. Christianity was once about human fallibility, about the worthlessness of all earthly expectations. Now it is seemingly preoccupied with human capabilities. It is a very great change.

2 | *Ministers of change*

'I find myself, unlike the contemporary Church, thinking more and more about the next world and less and less about the third world.' These words were written, shortly before his death last year, by Alexander Dru, the author and journalist.[1] It must be said, however, that his inclinations were indeed against the trend. Christianity today is preoccupied with political and social change throughout the world. But Christianity today is also notable for its lack of a distinctly *Christian* attitude towards the world it wishes to see changed. It has increasingly borrowed its political outlook and vocabulary, the issues it regards as most urgently requiring attention, and even its tests of moral virtue, from the progressive thinking of the surrounding secular culture.

The radical Christianity of the developing world, to which appeals are now so often made by western churchmen, in their call for change, is very familiar. For radical Christians of the Third World are not the wretched of the earth, but members of the bourgeois élite, emotionally attached to the idealism of social change. Their radicalism is itself a class characteristic of disaffected elements within the intelligentsia. Dr Sheila Cassidy, the British doctor imprisoned in Chile for failing to report medical treatment she had given to a fugitive, has recorded that the revolutionaries she met in detention were — as she put it — 'not desperate, oppressed peasants, but university students or young professionals from middle class families.'[2] It is likely that all political change ultimately derives from the agitation of élites. The World Council of Churches certainly

exemplifies such a process, for its officials, and the expert
opinion it consults, are clearly more advanced in their
politicization, and their preparedness to identify
Christianity with political change, than the members of
the constituent Churches. What is needed, according to the
1975 Report of one of its Commissioners, entitled *To
Break the Chains of Oppression,* is 'a vanguard of leaders',
the 'agents of change', They will be — again in the words
of the Report — 'the intellectual members of the élite,
students etc...' [3] Perhaps even more frankly stated is the
opinion of Dr Philip Potter, General Secretary of the
World Council of Churches: 'any movement for change
would always be in a minority,' he has said, 'because
people don't want change.'[4] Yet the World Council denies
that it is more radical than its own member Churches.[5] It
regards its support for the forces of political change in the
world as an act of solidarity with the world's oppressed, as
a symbol of its desire to abandon the dominance of western ways of thinking and to respect the resurgent cultures
of the developing world.[6] But in reality the world advance
of western cultural and political values was never more
successful than at the present time. They are conveyed in
the advances made by Marxism and in the creation,
through the capitalism of multinational corporations, of
consumer societies. The élitist radicalism of the World
Council of Churches is itself a purveyor of western values.
For what appears to western liberals as the Third World's
rejection of western cultural ideals is, on the contrary, the
adoption in the developing world of exactly the criticism
of western values that western liberals have themselves
made. The Third World has faithfully reproduced the cate-
chism of social change picked up from its western educators. The Third World Churches most noted for their radical politics are precisely the ones most open to the radical
liberalism and Marxist categorizing now so frequently en-

countered in the ecumenical circles of the developed nations.

To take this view of the mechanics of the present impulses for change is not, of course, to deny the validity of some of the ideals that are actually promoted by Christian organizations. The close relationship of religious and secular thinking in social and political issues does, however, raise some difficulties. Principally, the adoption of Humanist moral attitudes by Christian theologians in the 1960's meant that the view of man and his temporal expectations, once greatly at variance between secular Humanism and Christianity, became more or less the same. The result is the contemporary Christian insistence that the faith has essentially to do with 'human liberation'. The fact that this belief is derived from secular thought is actually acknowledged by the theologians. They do not see any difficulty; for by the simple device of regarding the progressive ideals furnished by their class background and cultural outlook as evidences of the Divine at work 'in the secular', they are able to promote the new Humanism as an authentic theological development. Of all the shifts in Christian thinking in modern times, this is by far the most radical in its effects. And it is not confined to the most progressive Churchmen, but is found in varying degrees of acceptance in the minds of many influential Christians today. Indeed, the word *ecumenical* itself has changed its meaning, and is now used by the World Council of Churches to mean, not just fellowship within the different Christian bodies, but within the entire human race.[7] To many ordinary believers, outside the circles of leadership and influence, modern developments seem to suggest that the Churches are 'little concerned to preserve the Christian heritage and deeply committed to radical change in national and international society.'[8]

There are some very considerable consequences of a

situation in which both the social and political morality of Christianity are derived directly from secular thought. For a start, material tests are applied to political virtue. Arrangements of human society are increasingly approved by Christianity when they attend most equitably, as it seems, to the material expectations of men. Thus organized Christianity is sometimes found on the side of Marxist movements for change — where the political alternatives, or the existing order, though allowing occasions for the cultivation of independent thought or enterprise, are considered, from the point of view of material reward, unjust. This tendency is actually assisted by 'the standard Marxist vocabulary' used in ecumenical circles.[9] 'Sometimes', wrote Dr Eugene Carson Blake, when he was General Secretary of the World Council of Churches, in 1972, 'sometimes it seems that of all secular philosophies Marxism is becoming the most popular and pervasive among our people.'[10] The reason is clear. Throughout the world, Marxism is becoming the form that the moral seriousness of the intelligentsia is taking in our day. The Churches, once again, reflect the solidarity of the high-minded in their enthusiasm for humanity. The practical result, in recent years, has been a large measure of Christian sympathy for Marxist movements seeking the replacement of the existing order in areas of South-East Asia, Southern Africa, and Latin America. This sympathy, furthermore, is often founded upon an uncritical acceptance of the propaganda depiction of social misery and economic deprivation which international Marxist agencies employ in order to enlist liberal support for the moral condemnation of capitalist societies everywhere. And because Christian leaders tend to amateurism in the very professional business of political tactics, and because they really are so properly dedicated to humanitarian ideals, they are permanently liable to absorb seemingly any account of world conditions which

exploits their generosity. They rationalize the political
intentions of others, in the selection of particular issues for
agitation. They make a simple, and generally innocent,
conflation of Christian love of neighbour with the most
hard-line Marxist devices to engineer radical social change.
They represent the political rhetoric of Marxism as merely
a succinct manner of expressing agreed moral truths about
human society. And so the Marxists' liturgy of propaganda
gets reproduced in the world views of Christianity.[11] A
government or social system marked down for replacement is first described in isolation, without reference to
the conditions general among mankind — and especially
the conditions in the socialist countries of the developing
world — in order to show the economic sufferings of the
poor under 'capitalism.' Ordinary security arrangements
are described as the trappings of a police state. This pattern of political criticism has preceded all the revolutions
of recent years. It is found, intact, in the views of the contemporary Church, where its repetition, drawn straight
from the secular political groups who invent and promote
it, is known as 'prophetic' discernment. The result is to
place Christianity among the leading influences making for
the demoralization of received western values throughout
the world. Dr David Owen, the British Foreign Secretary,
has recently observed: 'History has shown that the Christian critique of Communism has been one of the strongest
checks to its advancement'. [12] But that is ceasing to be the
case.

Now some of the social criticism may be true, and
aspects of Marxist social analysis are extremely valuable.
What is needed is extensive professional knowledge of
political theory and practice, and the will to see the virtues
as well as the faults of non-socialist patterns of social
organization. A sense of the ultimate worthlessness of
human expectations of a better life on earth — the very

thing religion ought to provide — is also lacking in our day. Unlike the Prince-bishops and clerical administrators of the past, whose political Christianity was highly developed, and whose political knowledge and skills were accordingly extensive and professional, the modern leaders of Christian opinion are too far removed from the real centres of political experience to be effective or accurate in their political judgment. And those Christians who *are* professionally accomplished are approved of selectively. It was Mr Michael Manley, the Prime Minister of Jamaica, therefore, whom the World Council of Churches chose to give an address at the Nairobi Assembly in 1975. In his speech — which the official Church of England report described as 'a major piece of political analysis'[13] — he denounced capitalism and parliamentary democracy, and contended for what he called 'true peoples' democracy.'[14]

The preparedness of Christian opinion to follow the diagnosis of world issues propagated by interested political agencies was amply illustrated by responses to the Chilean *coup* in 1973, which overthrew the Marxist government of Salvador Allende. It was, by contemporary standards, a pretty normal *coup*. The bloodshed and the ferocity of the security measures employed by General Pinochet's military junta have been exceeded in the advent of socialist régimes to South Vietnam, Cambodia, Angola and Afghanistan. But it is Chile that has continued to be condemned by the Churches. Why is this?

Chile has been especially singled out by Marxist groups as a likely case for attracting liberal opinion to the socialist cause. The economic chaos and the illegalities of the Allende administration are played down, and the military government — which is anyway far from being the model which capitalism would itself have selected for a set-piece defence — is depicted as the worst type of fascist dictatorship.[15] The Churches have accepted the main points in this propaganda version of the situation in Chile. During the Allende government, some fifteen thousand Communist activists gravitated to the country from other parts of Latin America, and these were the first to be expelled after the *coup*. Within forty-eight hours the World Council of Churches had been in touch with Christian groups in Chile to organize relief aid for these Communist refugees.[16] In a published appeal, the World Council regretted that what it called 'a unique social experiment' — by which it meant Allende's attempt to construct a Marxist society — had been extinguished.[17] The Council also involved itself with the formation of the Churches' *Committee of Cooperation for Peace in Chile* — an organization which, though largely concerned with social work, was highly political in outlook, preparing, as it announced, 'the way to human liberation.'[18] I have asked Dwain C. Epps, of the Commission of the Churches on International Affairs, how it was possible for the Chilean Churches to have acted so swiftly to help those whom they regarded as the victims of the *coup*. He attributed it to 'the work of the Holy Spirit'.[19] I would myself attribute it to the advanced politicization that the Churches had already undergone during the Allende period. One of the Churches which had not absorbed the prevalent social radicalism of the Chilean intelligentsia was the tiny Anglican Church — which has continued to be a consistent supporter of the military government.[20] It is therefore rather surprising to find that the Church of England was among those which adopted the standard left-wing analysis of the Chilean situation. It claimed that its views on Chile expressed support for humanitarian work rather than political opinion — but that is just a committee-style rationalization; an equivocation. The Church's official report on Chile, published in 1976, in describing what it called 'the characteristics of the military regime', referred to 'a fierce repression of the mass of the population' and 'economic repression.' 'Politically', the report declared, 'Chile today is a police state.'[21] Those read to me like ordinary political judgments, and ones, furthermore, which breathe the authentic air of international radical thinking. When the General Synod of the Church of England proceeded to announce its sympathy for those whom it described as 'the oppressed' in Chile[22], which it did in February 1976, the Reverend Paul Oestreicher, Chairman of Amnesty International, went out of his way to make it clear that the Synod was supporting the Chile Committee for Human Rights, a relief agency, with Archbishop Ramsey as a sponsor. It was not to be confused, he said, with the Chile Solidarity Campaign, 'an unashamedly left-wing organization supporting the former régime of Dr Allende', as he put it.[23] Meanwhile, in the same month, the Church of England's Board of Education, an institution under the direction of the Synod, sent out a propaganda advertisement published by the Chile Solidarity Campaign, the 'unashamedly left-wing organization.' As one might pour oil upon a fire, furthermore, it was sent to chaplains in higher education.[24] Of such political ineptitude is the new Kingdom of Heaven.

The contemporary Christian habit of representing ordinary political preferences as acts of 'prophecy' necessarily involves similar hazards. In 1968 the Fourth Assembly of the World Council of Churches, meeting in Uppsala, reported that 'no structures — ecclesiastical, industrial, governmental or international — lie outside the scope of the Churches' task as they seek to carry out their prophetic role in understanding the will of God for all men.'[25] But the content of their 'prophecy' inevitably seems to coincide with the propaganda models of radical liberalism and Marxism. Churchmen who become aware of this do not seem to find it incongruous. Thus Dr Philip Potter believes that 'it has been the secular writers and politicians who have been the prophets of our time.' He went on to cite the Black Power leaders Stokeley Carmichael and Malcolm X, who, he said, 'have given far more clear and powerful expression to the true meaning of the right hand of God than the Churches.'[26] Sometimes Christian acts of 'prophecy' are overtaken by events. In 1971, for example, a conference of Christians meeting in Tanzania were told that, in the struggle of the African liberation movements, there would never be the need to import foreign guerrilla fighters, because it was impossible to 'import a revolution.'[27] Today, it is black Christian leaders who welcome the Cuban presence in Africa. In 1972, the Church Missionary Society, in a fulsome appraisal of the progress Uganda could expect under General Amin, hailed his personal involvement in 'reconciling' a dispute over ecclesiastical jurisdiction as 'a true miracle of the Holy Spirit.'[28] Perhaps, in the circumstances, it was.

One of the most striking developments of the last twenty years has been the way in which all the Churches — Catholic, Orthodox, Protestant — have responded in about the same degree to the secular political ideologies. There are, in consequence, for the first time in history, no enormous differences in the social priorities of the major Churches. The only significant modification to this is the difference of emphasis imposed by the division between those who have adapted to the Marxist socialism of the eastern European bloc, and those who have absorbed the liberal social radicalism, with all its Marxist rhetoric, of the west and of the developing world. The Vatican, with its authoritative background of social teachings,[29] and its diplomatic professionalism,[30] is the most restrained and generalized in its pronouncements, though these are plainly reformist in tone and intention. It is from the Catholic hierarchies in individual countries or areas — like the Latin American Conference of bishops, or the Synod of bishops who meet periodically in Rome — that the really far-reaching political statements come. But it is the organization of the Protestants and the Orthodox, the World Council of Churches, that most specifically engages in the detailed application of contemporary political doctrines. The World Council, with its centralized bureaucracy,[31] and its 271 affiliated religious organizations, has a powerful Central Committee on which the representatives of the Third World and the Marxist countries now outnumber those from the western and capitalist states.[32]

The year 1968, which saw the peak of social protest by the western bourgeois radicals, also saw the corresponding excitement of the Christian leadership. It was the heady year of the student upheavals and the anti-Vietnam war demonstrations. In the Catholic Church, the first-fruits of the Encyclical *Populorum Progressio* of the preceding year, with its call for 'bold transformations' to secure a redistribution of the world's wealth,[33] came with the Medellín Conference of the Latin American bishops in 1968. There they condemned 'neo-colonialism',[34] called for the education of the masses into an awareness of their exploitation by capitalism,[35] and endorsed the need for 'new and reformed' political and economic structures.[36] Marxist vocabulary was freely used to describe the necessary changes. In 1968, also, the World Council of Churches gathered for its Fourth Assembly at Uppsala. The delegates declared that 'the political and economic structures groan under the burden of grave injustice,'[37] and urged the peoples of the world 'to realise the need for revolutionary change.'[38] The youth rebellion of the times was welcomed as a sign of political maturity.[39] That particular theme appeared at the Lambeth Conference, also held in 1968. Youth protest, the Anglican bishops of the world noticed, 'sounds an authentic note of criticism recalling Christians to obedience to the gospel.'[40] 'In the struggle for justice and freedom', the Anglicans resolved, 'the Church must be deeply involved in the search on the part of some for nationhood; in indigenous movements for the transformation of society; in dialogue with Marxists and humanists as well as with those others who control power structures.'[41] The official Christian statements of 1968 were, altogether, a very remarkable testimony to the close proximity of Church leaders to the intellectual and moral fashions of the time. With considerable passion — and only ten years ago — they adhered the Christian religion to what seemed to them to be enduring truths. Now they look like period pieces. So will today's political enthusiasms appear, in the years that are to come.

It is the apparent political bias of the World Council of Churches that has tarnished its image in the western press.[42] In this connexion, two things need to be borne in mind. First, the political involvement of the World Council forms only a part — if an increasing part — of its total ecumenical work. Secondly, the bad press in the western world has to be set against the growing good-will shown towards the World Council within the developing countries. Stimulated by the 1960 United Nations Declaration on Colonialism,[43] the Council rapidly advanced into the sponsorship of what the Uppsala Assembly described as 'movements for radical structural changes',[44] and, more idealistically still, 'for moving with history towards the coming of the new humanity.'[45] At the Bangkok Assembly, in 1973, the Council protested vigorously against what it categorized as 'the tragic shame of the Indochina War' and 'the bloody suppression of liberation movements'.[46] Political involvement has not been merely academic. In 1972 the Council encouraged the Ethiopian Orthodox Church in a programme designed to 'animate' priests for social change. At least two hundred underwent the special course, and it was they who took part in the 1974 left-wing demonstrations in Addis Ababa.[47] The longer term consequences of their labours have subsequently become evident. In 1975, a World Council Commission described the distribution of wealth throughout the world as 'organized theft',[48] and argued for what it called 'a revolutionary process' to change it.[49] The Fifth Assembly of the Council, at Nairobi in 1975, took as its theme 'Jesus Christ Frees and Unites' — a phrase which hints at the notions of liberation and solidarity that abound in the world movements for radical change.

These sorts of affirmation are easily rationalized away as merely the sentiments of humanitarianism. But in the context in which they are formulated, and in view of the politically suggestive language in which they are expressed, there cannot be much doubt about their actual pedigree. Officials of the World Council admit that the staff are 'nearly all socialists'.[50] Everyone thinks the same way about almost everything. As Dr Kenneth Slack, former General Secretary of the British Council of Churches, has written: 'For all the vaunting of the method of dialogue as a way towards truth and understanding there is too little evidence of provision of contrasting viewpoints.'[51] The World Council is clearly selective in its condemnation of supposed injustices. It was, for example, a consistent opponent of American policy in South Vietnam,[52] even going so far as to give financial assistance to American deserters.[53] The Council also has a long record of refusing to criticize Communist governments, arguing that its private representations are more effective.[54] In its considerable involvements with Human Rights issues, too, there is evidence of left-ward political inclinations. In 1971 the Churches' Commission on International Affairs drafted a statement on Human Rights intended — in their own words — to 'move beyond the western liberal interpretation that views individual rights as supreme, to give emphasis to collective rights.'[55] That, as it happens, is the Marxist position on Human Rights, and the version eventually adopted by the Central Committee of the World Council was discreetly less explicit.[56]

But it has been the Programme to Combat Racism, begun in 1969, which has most fostered the impression that the World Council is politically biassed. Here, as elsewhere in its policies, spokesmen are able to point out that to have done nothing would have itself been a political act — an acceptance of the political arrangements of the *status quo*.[57] Similarly in defence of the controversial grants to the guerrilla fighters of the 'liberation movements', first made from the Special Fund in 1970, the Council invoked the doctrine of 'institutionalized violence' to show that the defenders of the existing political order use violent means to maintain it.[58] The grants to 'liberation movements', mostly in Southern Africa, which in August 1978 included one of £43,000 to Rhodesian Patriotic Front guerrillas, have raised general questions about the Christian use of force for political objectives;[59] but in the end attitudes towards the policy depend upon individual political preference. To some, the guerrillas are freedom fighters; to others, merely terrorists. More difficult to view dispassionately is the World Council's insistence that the grants are made for humanitarian purposes only,[60] since it is clear that money made available to the insurgents, by relieving them of the necessity to purchase medical supplies, and so forth, can be expended on armaments.[61] In such a situation it is a species of dishonesty to hide behind a technicality in supporting revolutionary change.

A further problem with the programme is its selectivity. Racism is almost universal, but the Council's policy is solely directed at white racism. Bishop Kenneth Sansbury has described the reason in these words: 'White racism, just because it finds expression in social, economic and political structures, was seen to be the most dangerous.'[62] No less controversial than the grants to 'liberation movements', though less well-known, have been a succession of smaller allocations to such causes as the 'Malcolm X Liberation University' in the United States,[63] and a militant Black Power Marxist organization in England.[64] In such matters, the political bias of the World Council surely loses all disguise. And in some smaller things, too. During the Nairobi Assembly, in 1975, groups of delegates went off to visit the slum shanty-towns at the edge of the city — where about a third of the population actually live.[65] None of them appear to have used the experience as evidence of political injustice, calling down anathemas upon the régime. For Kenya is black Africa. Visits by Christian activists to comparable slums in South Africa or Chile are made the basis of extravagant condemnations of the political systems that allow them. But those are countries whose governments are for other, political reasons earmarked for destruction. That is the difference.

3 | A new Commandment : Human Rights

The present relationship between Christianity and the ideals of Western liberalism is an extremely close one. There is no great dissimilarity between secular and religious outlooks on moral questions, as there has been in the past: the ideas which now characterize the moral seriousness of educated opinion are found faithfully reproduced in the discourse of the Churches. This is nowhere more plainly seen than in the support given by institutional Christianity to the prevalent enthusiasm for Human Rights. It is, indeed, more than support merely — the Churches have come to regard Human Rights as something like fundamental Christianity.

There is not, of course, anything new about the involvement of Christianity with Human Rights doctrines. The idea that certain immutable freedoms should be reserved from the interference of government was taken over from Greek philosophy and incorporated into medieval scholastic thinking. In St. Thomas Aquinas, a complicated hierarchy of divine and natural laws was described very explicitly, and at the Reformation both sides appealed to natural rights in order to justify their attempts at exterminating each other. Recent Christian statements in support of Human Rights have acknowledged their indebtedness to this earlier tradition of natural law, and the Church of England's view, expressed a year ago in the amazing economy of an eighteen-page pamphlet — wherein two thousand years of political speculation are summarized[1] — is in fact extremely traditionalist in its insistence on old natural law precepts about the limitations of government.

Now the present ideology of Human Rights in western thinking illustrates two leading difficulties with classical formulations of natural law. First, arguments about society, government and individual rights, based upon natural law, assume an unimpeachable moral authority, true for all time; yet the *content* of what men choose to regard as natural rights is unstable. It is a matter of record that seemingly any claim to personal choice is capable of being represented as a natural law right. The second difficulty is that natural law claims are by nature *political*. Men sanctify their ordinary political preferences, drawn from the ephemeral political cultures of their day, and regard them as embodiments of fundamental law. The recent tendency towards the politicization of moral values has joined these two aspects of natural law applications together and the result, in the contemporary Human Rights movement, has elevated Western liberalism to the apparent authority of eternal truth. And the scale is a large one, for Human Rights claims have now become the central motive of those concerned with changing the entire basis of the world order. Western democracies urge these sorts of moral objection in their critiques of authoritarian régimes, of both left and right. Socialist states respond with exactly the same rhetoric of Human Rights in their rejection of western liberalism. There is a shared vocabulary of Human Rights, but the content varies according to ideology or class.[2] Natural law, as in the past, is proving to be a universal dissolvent of order. The world is a more dangerous place — as ideological differences are always more bloody than differences inspired by conflicting material interests.

I am not, I need hardly say, arguing that many of the personal freedoms now being sought within Human Rights terms of reference are not to be desired. Many are. It is just that the sort of ultimate claims employed to make them authentic are defective. The content of natural law is

quite arbitrary. Western liberalism locates it in individualism. It regards the state as by definition the regulator of a
pluralism of social and moral values — as inherently unable
to decide final truth for its citizens, and so it offers them a
set of supposedly basic freedoms upon whose foundations
they may construct a private enterprise morality. Socialist
states, in contrast, do regard themselves as the embodiment of ethical truth. They are the creation of a single
ideology, and the doctrine of Human Rights is, for them,
collective rather than individualistic.[3] Here, then, at the
very beginning of any consideration of the nature of
Human Rights, is a fundamental difference in the way
they are understood between the two major political
groupings into which the modern world is arranged. As it
happens, western liberalism is a good deal less 'open' about
its interior values than it supposes — and frequently gives
legislative force to moral ideas which clash with individual
preference. The British race relations laws illustrate this,
for example. In fact, liberalism is very dogmatic about the
morality it promotes; it is just that it lacks institutional
coherence.

Christian involvement with Human Rights ideology does
not result from a remembered deposit of traditional adhesion by the Churches to natural laws, however. Their contemporary concern takes its inspiration from general
developments of secular opinion — the emphasis on
Humanism by the intelligentsia in the 1960's, with its
enthusiastic incorporation into theology; the Helsinki
Conference on European Security and Cooperation in
1975; and the priority given to Human Rights in the world
outlook of President Carter. Not in rhetoric and content
only, but also in chronology, the Christian passion for
Human Rights exactly corresponds to the development of
ideas within the western intelligentsia as a whole. Yet the
Churches now see Human Rights as the essence of the

Christian message. 'The Church', according to one of the documents uttered by the Second Vatican Council, 'by virtue of the Gospel entrusted to her, proclaims man's rights and acknowledges and esteems the modern movement to promote these rights everywhere.'[4] The World Council of Churches, a decade later, in the more precise language which represents the escalation of Human Rights ideology, has declared: 'The struggle of Christians for human rights is a fundamental response to Jesus Christ. That Gospel leads us to become ever more active in identifying and rectifying violations of human rights in our socities.'[5] In the same year, 1975, the World Council published a practical handbook entitled *How to File Complaints of Human Rights Violations.*[6] The Human Rights movement, ostensibly concerned with the cultivation of moral opinion, was rapidly becoming political. Given the terms of reference, the transformation was perhaps unavoidable.[7] 'The struggle for human rights is inevitably a political activity', as Niall MacDermott, Secretary General of the International Commission of Jurists, told the Catholic Institute for International Relations in 1976.[8] In the words, again, of the World Council of Churches, Christian work for Human Rights now meant 'work at the most basic level towards a society without unjust structures.'[9] And that is a basic political definition.

The identification of Christianity with Human Rights ideology, in fact, is the contemporary manifestation of a permanent phenomenon — the adoption by the Church leadership, in each successive generation, of the moral and political idealism of the surrounding secular culture. And, as in all previous examples, theologians and Christian publicists have adjusted traditional understandings of religious doctrine in order to represent the canons of contemporary moral seriousness as exactly embodying the spirit of the Gospels. The Human Rights movement also provides the content of much of the present politicization of Christianity. It identifies the Church with the moral sanctions claimed as the justification for the goals of western liberalism — whose transient moral enthusiasms are, in characteristic bourgeois manner, represented as eternal verities. The aims of Human Rights campaigns are being given the authority of the laws of God. I want to show the difficulties this development raises in relation to the debate about Human Rights in the Soviet Union — especially as it affects attitudes to religious liberty. For in this context the matter appears sharp and clear to most western observers: the Soviet Union is widely taken to illustrate the violation of fundamental religious freedoms.

Western concern about the restrictions placed upon the exercise of religion in the Soviet Union once expressed opposition to Marxist atheism. Now it is expressed in the language of Human Rights. The effect is actually the same: what looks to western Christians like a simple demand for the free expression of opinion appears to Soviet observers as political objection to the ethical basis of Marxist society. And there is, indeed, some validity in that, since the Human Rights movement in the west *is* politicized and *does* seek the extension of the ideals of western bourgeois liberalism. Official Russian Church leaders deny that there is any violation of Human Rights in the Soviet Union, or that legal restrictions on religion are harmful — an embarrassment recognized by the Archbishop of Canterbury after his return from Moscow in October last year. 'The issue is a very difficult one to sum up', he then remarked at a press conference.[10]   During the visit, he had raised a number of individual cases of alleged discrimination against Christian believers, and this had in effect symbolized the incorporation of the question of religious liberty in the Soviet Union into the list which the western liberals regard as basic Human Rights issues.[11]   There is also considerable attention paid in the west to religious *samizdat* literature[12] — unofficial writings and journals privately circulated by dissidents, many of them reporting individual cases of what are taken to be Human Rights violations.[13] This sort of literature is of very uneven quality, some of it plainly expressing genuine grievances, but a lot of it inspired by conscious or unconscious rejection of the ethical basis of the Soviet State. Again, some of the writers are clearly motivated by anti-Russian nationalism — as in the tracts from the Baltic States, and especially from Catholic Lithuania[14] — and some others represent an antiquated repugnance to scientific ideas.[15] Modern religious dissent in the Soviet Union originated in opposition to the policy of official Christian leaders, Orthodox, Baptist and Catholic, who have registered their Churches under the requirements of the 1929 Law of Religious Associations, and so have accepted the principle of State supervision.[16] It is a protest against what seems to be a compromise with atheism.[17]

This impression has been reinforced by the Soviet government's policy of supporting the official churches against the dissenters[18] — especially in 1961, when acceptance of greater state control over congregations resulted in secessions from both the Russian Orthodox and the Baptist Churches.[19] Some of the religious dissidents do actually regard themselves as loyal to the Soviet system,[20] but a marked feature of some of the most well-reported groups has been their advanced politicization — usually taking the form of adhesion to western liberal concepts of Human Rights.[21] The most distinguished representative of this tendency is Alexander Solzhenitsyn, with his insistence on the relationship between liberal individualism and religious belief,[22] and his hope of a future Russian state, free of Marxism, embodying the moral order inherent in the Orthodox faith.[23] Levitin-Krasnov, another prominent opponent of the present leadership of the Orthodox church, became 'the chief link between Orthodox dissent and the civil rights movement'[24] when he joined the 'Action Group for the defence of Human Rights in the Soviet Union' in 1969. Most of those who articulate their opposition to the state obey its laws; but a few do not, appealing, instead, to the higher demands, as they see it, of religious conscience — and these are sometimes prosecuted and imprisoned.[25] It is their cases which usually form the basis of the erroneous impression, widespread in the west, that the expression of religious belief as such results in legal penalties. The opinions of some dissidents are such that they would be likely to face prosecution in most countries. In 1967 and 1968, for example, a number of dissident intellectuals went on trial in Leningrad charged with anti-Soviet activities. They belonged to a group called the 'All-Russian Social Christian Alliance for Liberation of the People.' Though apparently represented by some in the west as an ordinary Human Rights organization,[26] they in fact seem to have stood for white supremacy, anti-semitism, and the establishment, by force, of a neo-Fascist state structure.[27]

What, then, is the position of the Church in the Soviet Union, and does it legitimately come within the list of violated Human Rights? By Lenin's Decree of 1918 Church and State were separated and the freedom either to profess or not to profess religious faith was guaranteed. Article 52 of the new Constitution of the Soviet Union, adopted in 1977, preserves this freedom and also defines the right 'to conduct religious worship or atheistic propaganda.'[28] In the words of Nikolai Zabolotsky, Study Secretary of the World Council of Churches Unit on Justice and Service, and formerly on the staff of the Leningrad Theological Seminary, 'it is very noble of our government to give this recognition to a minority group like the

Church.'[29] Indeed, it can be said that religion is the only non-Marxist ideology which is officially tolerated in the Soviet Union.[30] But the restrictions are also very extensive. Churches have to be registered and to supply the names of members to the State; the religious education of children is prohibited, though parents may give private instruction; no religious activity is permitted outside church buildings, and charitable or social work is not allowed because the State regards itself as providing adequate welfare facilities.[31] In practice, therefore, and as the new Constitution makes clear, religious liberty amounts to the right of public worship — in churches which are leased to the congregation, without charge, by the State. It is a very fundamental right, because in the Orthodox Church, to which the overwhelming majority of the thirty million professed Christians in the Soviet Republics owe their allegiance,[32] the performance of the Sacred Liturgy is not just a corporate expression of belief: it unfolds the very essence of the unchanging mysteries of transcendence — it is the disclosure of celestial truth, the very nature of Christianity itself.[33] Contemporary western Christians, who change their services around according to fashion or personal inclination, undervalue the significance of this freedom of worship. Western Christianity has so redefined its meaning in terms of social activism that it cannot comprehend a Church which is satisfied with the mere performance of worship. But the Russian Orthodox Church is satisfied.

In practice, there is constant vigilance by the State to keep the Church within its designated sphere. Provided that is respected, there is acknowledged to be a free competition between Marxism and religion for the souls of the population, or — and this is a heavy qualification — as free a competition as the unequal muscle of the two contenders will allow. Opinions differ along ideological lines as to whether there are real violations by the State of the guarantees written into the Constitution.[34] The Soviet authorities themselves, aware of some reported cases, passed legislation in 1966 which made discrimination against religious believers a criminal offence.[35] Dissidents have frequently complained of state interference over the parental rights of religious instruction, for example, or of discrimination against believers in jobs or in higher education. Secret instructions are said to be issued to local officials by the Council for Religious Affairs, the central supervising body set up in 1965, which introduce an arbitrary element into the legal position of religion.[36] But cases are very difficult to authenticate, and the Orthodox clergy deny that they have any real substance. Allegations of interference with worship are very rare, and the closure of ten thousand churches during Khruschev's rigorous application of the laws on religion, early in the 1960's, has been defended by the Metropolitans of both Moscow and Leningrad, on the grounds that the churches were anyway redundant, due to a decline in Church attendance.[37] Relative to the size of the populations, that is to say, the number of redundant churches in Russia is comparable to figures for Western European countries. The influence of Marxism may not even be the determining factor in the decline of religion in the Soviet Union. As in the west, it is associated with urbanization and the consequent secularization of values. It is Russian Church officials who may be responsible for something else which is often taken, in the west, as state interference with religion — the ban on the import of Bibles. In January of this year, Moscow Radio explained that the ban was imposed at the request of the Patriarch of Moscow, who objected to the introduction of Bibles with texts that did not correspond to the canonical version allowed by the Orthodox Church.[38] Such cooperation of Church and State is, in the circumstances, an extraordinary testimony to the pragmatism of current applications of religious policy. At times, in fact, the favoured treatment accorded the Orthodox Church points to what Levitin-Krasnov has described as 'a strange paradox: a state church within a system of an atheist state.'[39]

It is, of course, still the intention of Marxist-Leninism to eradicate religious belief. For scientific socialism regards Christianity not just as a superstitious survival, but as false science. It is a rival understanding of the nature of men and of the laws of human society. Unlike the secularized west, where religion is increasingly considered a peripheral affair, whose claim to a unique view of man has even been abandoned by theologians themselves, Christianity is regarded by the Communist Party as a serious ideological adversary. According to Marxist-Leninist theory, it is not to be rooted out by force, but the social and economic conditions which generate it are to be eliminated. Existing believers are not to be coerced into a renunciation of their faith; they are to be persuaded by reason.[40] It is precisely the application of this doctrine that has led to sharp criticism by Albania,[41] a country which in 1971 declared itself to be 'the first atheist state in the world', and which closed down the Churches and shot the clergy. The Soviet Union employs educative means. Lessons in scientific atheism are held in the schools, and there is a compulsory course for students in higher education. Very large numbers of lectures and publications are provided in order to foster the eradication of what are called 'religious prejudices'.[42] These courses start with comparative religious studies and are intended to disprove the exclusive claims of the Churches by pointing to the primitive common source of all religious phenomenology. There is actually a marked similarity between this approach and the curricula proposed by many Christian educational theorists in Britain, who seek to end the exclusive teaching of Christianity in

the schools. They, too, regard religion as a social phenomenon, to be considered and discussed alongside alternative
so-called 'life-styles'. I pointed this out to the head of the
broadcasting section of the Council for Religious Affairs in
Moscow, but he seemed incredulous — unable to conceive
that capitalist society could treat its own values with such
abandon.[43] At least we do not as yet have museums of
atheism in the United Kingdom — like those in Leningrad and Kiev. The Leningrad museum[44] has in fact just
installed a new exhibit. It is a photograph of the Archbishop of Canterbury.

The Communist Party of the Soviet Union regards
atheism as inseparable from the other goals of socialism. It
is this fact which makes nonsense of the hopes that were
invested in the 'dialogue' between Christians and Marxists
in that last decade.[45] It has been, anyway, an exchange
largely among intellectuals, and mostly in the west. Within the Soviet Union the notion that both Christianity and
Marxism have now become so philosophically flexible that
they can explore mutual compatibilities[46] just appears as
an ideological monstrosity. They reject the whole basis of
the Christian Humanism that has dominated the Christian
side of the dialogue, and consider proposals from Euro-
communists — like Enrico Berlinguer's idea of a 'historic
compromise' between Catholics and Communists in
Italy[47] — as elementary departures from Marxist doctrine.
Nor is the assumption made by western liberal Christians
that a reformed, socially-progressive Christianity will pave
the way for an understanding with Communism likely to
prove valid. The Communist Party officially encourages
tactical cooperation with progressive Christians in order to
pursue its world policies[48]. But it actually regards reformed religion — particularly the variety which is loaded
with social concern — as even more dangerous than the
reactionary sort. For it tinkers with the superstructure

only, and gives the false impression that human advancement may be accomplished without a radical transformation of the means of production and exchange.[49] As
Charles Andras has remarked, 'many Christians who joined
the dialogue were extremely naive, without any previous
experience in the political field.'[50] The Communist state
regards itself as fully competent to decide about the
ethical basis of society, and it has decided that it shall be
established exclusively according to historical materialism.
It is as well to remember that Christianity once regarded itself as having such a competence to define truth and, like
the Communists today, it did not give ideological tolerance
to alternative systems of belief. The Soviet museums of
atheism contain vivid depictures of the Inquisition.

Within the confines allowed to them by the Soviet state,
most Christian leaders seem to find a satisfactory enough
space for the exercise of their faith. They are the first to
deny that official treatment of religion violates their
Human Rights. When the World Council of Churches,
meeting at Nairobi in 1975, was urged to include the
Soviet Union in the Assembly's statement on Human
Rights, the Russian Orthodox delegates protested at
once.[51] It is supposed, in the west, that this sort of action
is an expression of enlightened self-interest; that the
Russian churchmen are prudent enough to pay lip-service
to the dominant Soviet state rather than face a full assault
upon their churches.[52] But this does not appear to be the
case. Russian Christians support Soviet politics, at home as
well as abroad, because they believe them to be true.
Socialist values have become 'well embedded in the secular
ethic pronounced from the pulpit', according to the find-
ings of recent sociological investigation, 'and echoed by
wide sectors of ordinary believers'.[53] In a recent statement, the All-Union Council of Evangelical Christians
criticized foreigners who accused the Soviet state of violat-

ing Human Rights, and declared themselves to be, as they said 'flesh of the flesh of their people who are building a society based on the principles of social justice.'[54] In February of this year, Metropolitan Aleksii of Tallinn and Estonia wrote that 'all religious associations in the Soviet Union have every opportunity to carry out their mission freely and in accordance with Church traditions.'[55] Ever since the Orthodox joined the World Council of Churches in 1961, they have consistently used that forum for the promotion of Soviet foreign policy.[56] In the great Orthodox seminary at Zagorsk, you may see the medals presented to the Patriarch by the Soviet State in recognition of his work for peace: an indication of the extent of the involvement of Russian Church leaders in the Soviet-inspired international peace movement, a further means by which Communist foreign policy ideals are propagated.[57] Quite apart from this association of Christianity with socialism, there is another reason why the Russian Church finds itself reasonably happy with its present position. Orthodoxy and patriotism have always been closely linked: during the last war, for example, there was a resurgence of popular religiosity elicited by the Church's identification of the faith with the campaign against Fascism. It led Stalin to relax some of the religious restrictions.[58] Church and State have always been related: indeed, the controls exercised over the Church by the secular administrators of Tsarist Russia were sometimes scarcely less rigorous than the present ones.[59] Echoes of this historical link can still be heard even in today's changed political circumstances. Religious dissidents claim that the official Church leadership loses the respect of the people through its support of Soviet ideals,[60] but most available evidence seems to point to almost exactly the opposite conclusion.[61]

The consensus within the western churches that identifies Christianity and Human Rights therefore runs into difficulty when it is applied — as it so often is — to the religious situation in the Soviet Union. Russian Christians agree that Human Rights are important, but they disagree with Western Christians both about their nature and their present form in the world. This should impose caution upon those prepared to define Christianity in terms of the content of Human Rights. As there is no agreement about the content, at least between Christians in east and west — and actually also, on closer examination, among western Christians themselves — the practice of adding religious authority to moral and political campaigns for Human Rights is both divisive and partial. In reality, Human Rights issues become the means by which Christians express their endorsement of the political values of their own societies. It is all very relative to time and circumstance.

4 | *The imperialism of political religion*

'Christ was a great revolutionary.' So Fidel Castro declared during his visit to Jamaica last year, adding that he saw no incompatibility between Christianity and Cuban socialism.[1] In 1970, just after his election as President of Chile, another Marxist, Salvador Allende, observed that the Catholic Church had 'changed fundamentally.' In fact he saw it now as being, as he put it, 'in our favour'. And of his Marxist alliance he said: 'we are going to try to make a reality out of Christian thought.'[2]

These extraordinary remarks testify to the very considerable shifts of emphasis that have occurred within South American Christianity in the last two decades; they point to changes which are only imperfectly appreciated in western society. This lack of understanding in part derives from the greater preparedness of western Christians to listen to the views of Latin American ecclesiastical progressives than to the opinions of the more typical, institutionalized religious leadership. Christians of the developed world regard the Latin American radicals as authentically speaking for the oppressed and exploited of the Third World. But are they? It is indeed the case that South America is the only wholly Christian continent of the developing world. Yet despite some obviously unique features in recent Latin American religious history, there is a lot that is extremely familiar about the politicization of the progressive element in the Church – the part which has acquired so much influence both inside and outside South America. Much of their thinking, however, as elsewhere in politicized Christian circles, depends upon ideological presuppositions that are neither distinctively Christian nor Latin American. It may be none the worse for that. But Latin American Christianity does provide a very clear example of what happens when Christians accommodate the political values of surrounding opinion. In the 1930's and '40's, the Church leadership adopted the ideals of the European corporate state; in the 1950's they were attracted to 'Developments' social reform; in the 1960's they reflected the radical critique of capitalist society then common within the western intelligentsia; in the 1970's they have moved on to identify Christianity with the ideology of Human Rights.

There is, however, one feature which is peculiarly South American, and which explains many aspects of change in the Church quite independently of political activism. There is in the hemisphere, as everyone will tell you, a 'crisis of the Church'. So there is in the western developed nations. But here it is produced by the failure of the Churches to retain the support of the populations, by the impact of secularization, by the loss, among Christians themselves, of any distinct sense of the historical claims of Christianity. In Latin America, the 'crisis of the Church' is not caused by loss of faith — that is a phenomenon still restricted to sections of the intelligentsia.[3] There the crisis reflects the *confidence* of the Church, with its energetic adjustment to social transformations, and especially to its attempts to meet the chronic manpower shortage in its ministry. This is often lost on western Christian observers of the Latin American scene, who speak, in consequence, as if what South Americans themselves call *socialcristianismo* — the social and political interpretation of Christianity — was the decisive element in contemporary religious history. The really dramatic changes of the present 'crisis', however, are not produced by radical social theorizing but by flexible response to the changed social context in which the Church operates.

The most basic consideration here is the twentieth-century population explosion and the rapidly increasing mobility of people, the drift of the rural workers into the cities — creating the *barrio* or *poblaciones,* the shanty-towns of the poor, which are found around almost every large centre of population. The ecclesiastical parish has more or less broken down as an effective pastoral unit in very many places. It no longer corresponds to manageable, or even definable, social groups. Parishes in the north-east of Brazil — still one of the least developed areas in the continent — sometimes contain 40,000 to 50,000 souls; and in other places there may be as many as three parishes in the care of a single priest.[4] Vocations to the priesthood are fewer than you would expect in what is still a broadly Catholic culture, and foreign priests, from Europe and North America, are brought in on a large scale. In countries like Bolivia and Brazil, a third of the clergy are from overseas. Not surprisingly, this situation has led to extensive questioning of ecclesiastical structures and great readiness to experiment with new patterns of ministry. With the addition of some social theorizing, often imported by the foreign priests, this has now become the attempt to create what Church leaders call *Iglesia del pueblo* — the 'people's Church'.[5] Emphasis is placed on simplicity and austerity in clerical lifestyles and dress.[6] The atmosphere generated throughout the entire Catholic Church by the Second Vatican Council acts as a supplementary incentive to change. There are, as elsewhere in the world, radical liturgical experiments. Combined with the wish to create a 'people's Church', this has in South America resulted in amused newspaper references to the mass as 'misa a Gó Gó' and 'misa a la Gaucho.' The bishops of South America are now firmly committed to structural changes. Through the Council of Latin American bishops (CELAM), set up in 1955, with a permanent secretariat and a series of specialized commissions, the leadership of the Church has fashioned a unifying ecclesiastical organization, with markedly progressive sympathies.[7] Again, many of the staff priests working within this bureaucracy are foreigners.

There are, of course, considerable variations within the degree both of structural reform and of politicization within the Church: Chile has always been particularly advanced, and Colombia notably conservative, for example.[8] And, as elsewhere in the Christian world, the leadership tends to be considerably more progressive than the laity. But it is the foreign clergy who are everywhere noted for their radical politics and who are most forthright in expressing them. Indeed, much of what is taken by Western Christians as characteristically 'Latin American' Catholic thought turns out to be the influence of European and North American mission and staff priests.[9] The same is true of Protestantism — which suffers, in fact, from its association with North Americanism. It is a gringo religion.

The development of radical politics by the foreign clergy is well illustrated in the career of 'Paul Gallet', the pen-name of a French priest working in North-East Brazil from 1962. By March 1964, just before the right-wing military coup, he had come to hope for what he called 'a revolution like Cuba'.[10] Another, Protestant, example is provided by the Lutheran Bishop Helmut Frenz, banned from Chile by the military government in 1975. 'I became a highly politicized Christian', he later admitted; and added, 'class struggle is no Marxist propaganda; it is a reality.'[11] Bishop Frenz had been one of the presidents of the 'Committee for Cooperation for Peace' — the Chilean Human Rights agency — and an observer for the World Council of Churches. Apart from the foreign clergy themselves, the others most noticeable for their political radicalism are Latin Americans who have trained for the priesthood, or studied, abroad — especially at the European universities, and particularly at Louvain, in Belgium. There they picked up versions of Marxism from the bourgeois radical circles in which they mixed. Thus Camilo Torres, the Colombian priest who gave up the priesthood in order to work for the poor, as he put it, had studied social sciences at Louvain. There he met the Peruvian priest, Gustavo Gutiérrez, later to become the most distinguished of the Marxist theologians in South America.

But not all the foreign clergy, or those who have studied abroad, become left-wing by any means; it is simply that those who do get themselves listened to. Earlier, in 1978, I visited the working class *poblaciones* around Santiago, in Chile, and met some Italian priests, who run a home for deaf and dumb children in the district of Lampa. Neither they, nor any other priests working among the poor I heard about during the visit, were in any way politicized. But their love of the poor for whom they worked was among the most impressive things I have ever seen.

Social concern is not a new development within the leadership of South American Catholicism. In the 1930's and '40's it took the form of seeking to embody Papal teachings on social questions in the structure of the corporate state. The influence of Franco's Spain, Salazar's Portugal, and Mussolini's Italy were important in this. There has been some enduring influence, too. For much of the contemporary Christian criticism of liberal capitalism in Latin America — now rendered in Marxist language[12] — is a familiar echo from the rejection of capitalism made in the 'thirties by Fascism. The transition may be traced in the life of Dom Helder Camara, Archbishop of Recife in Brazil, and known, because of his small size and enormous energy, as 'the electric mosquito.' Camera is the only South American Catholic leader known to most western Christians. He is a highly politicized man — and always has been. He was a convinced Fascist as a young priest.[13] Now he is a convinced Socialist.

In the later 1950's and '60's, the Church leaders moved on to Christian democracy. This corresponded to the 'Developmentist' stage of Latin American politics: the conviction that underdevelopment could be overcome within existing but reformed social and political structures by capitalist economics and external aid. Yet within Christian Democracy — just as within the thinking of Western bourgeois radicalism in the 1960's — there grew up a sharp rejection of capitalist society. This is especially associated with Eduardo Frei, both during and after his term as Christian Democrat President of Chile. It could, indeed, be fairly remarked that in the now celebrated election of 1970 the social programme of the Christian Democrats was scarcely distinguishable from that of the successful Marxist candidate, Salvador Allende.[14] The transition to increasingly radical social teachings can be seen in the Pastoral Letters of the bishops of all the Latin American republics during the 1960's, their opinions more or less exactly corresponding to the adoption of social radicalism within the western intelligentsia in general. Extensive reforms in living conditions were more and more frequently linked to calls for structural political change. In some measure this was inspired by fear of Communism — buying off the revolution with reforms. But the main motive was a genuine shift to more radical ideology.[15] Even the evangelical Pentecostal churches have come to acquire a radical political position; an unusual illustration of the movement from 'sect' to 'church' type of religion, since their new radicalism is the characteristic not of the poor but of the affluent intelligentsia.

Both the development of radical social criticism, and the

renewed conflicts of Church and State that this has inaugurated in some Latin American countries in the present decade, have signalled a further development. This is the adoption by the Church of the pervasive enthusiasm for Human Rights which has grown within western liberal opinion during the 1970's. Conservative governments have attacked the Church for meddling in politics:[16] again, a classic sign of the politicization of religion. The Church has replied by insisting that its concern is not political but moral — and has spoken of Human Rights as something superior to the authority of the State. Christians have also argued that the clergy have been drawn into politics by the need to defend social justice in countries where the Church is the only free institution, the only independent voice.[17] Thus in Guatemala — a country with a long, nineteenth-century history of Church and State conflict — the clash between the bishops and the government over Human Rights in 1976 prompted the Vice-President to accuse the Church of political interference.[18] A similar pattern has recently appeared in Argentina, Bolivia, Paraguay, Nicaragua, El Salvador, and, above all, in Chile since the military coup in 1973. In Chile, Christian work for *Derechos Humanos* — Human Rights — has been deeply mixed up with political criticism of the government, leading to the detention or exile of many priests.[19] The ecumenical Committee of Cooperation for Peace, which was unambiguous in its condemnation of what it called 'the situation of oppression' in Chile,[20] was closed down by Cardinal Silva, Archbishop of Santiago, in 1975, after representatives from General Pinochet, President of Chile. He accused it of having become infiltrated by Marxists.[21] In 1976, the progressive attitudes of the Chilean bishops earned the approval of Moscow Radio:[22] a tribute, perhaps, of doubtful utility to their cause. The Church's voice remains something to be reckoned with. And when, in June last year, the Chilean Minister for Justice called the bishops 'stupid Marxists', he had to resign.[23]

In contrast to the progressive élite who dominate the thinking of South American Catholicism are the conservative majority. As in Europe and North America their ideas have failed to achieve respectable articulation; in fact they have often shown themselves to be lamentably ignorant of the subtleties in their opponents' positions. At that level, fear of Communism really *is* often advanced in opposition to all reform. Right-wing Catholic groups, like the Society for the Defence of Tradition, Family and Property, in Chile and Brazil, tend to reject even the most necessary alterations of the Church's pastoral function. And the promotion of politics for what are thought of as distinctly *Christian* reasons is not a monopoly of the left. The conservative military régimes that now govern so much of South America see themselves as the guardians of traditional Christian values and of Christian civilization. These claims often correspond to deeply-felt and popular instincts, expressed in nationalism.[24] Traditionalist Christians accuse the bishops of being too far ahead of public opinion, of listening to the intellectual left with too much respect.[25] In 1974 the Protestant Churches in Chile articulated opinions of the silent majority, when they publicly thanked the military for having saved the country from Marxism; and Bishop Helmut Frenz, the exiled Lutheran leader, is said to have lost the support of three-quarters of his Church membership as a result of his work for the Peace Committee.[26]

At the other end of the political spectrum is the small group of actively Marxist priests. Some of these, again, like the North American Maryknoll fathers who joined guerrilla forces in Central America, are foreigners.[27] The revolutionary priests have attracted a lot of overseas attention. Camilo Torres was 'better known in Paris than in Bogotá',

his home town, according to the Colombian press.[28]
Torres called for the formation of *Ejército de Liberación
Nacional* — a national army of liberation — to start a
'people's war' for the overthrow of the bourgeois state.[29]
Departing to the Colombian countryside to join a guerrilla
band, he was shot to death during an ambush at El Car-
men in 1966, and has since become something of a cult
figure, a sort of ecclesiastical Che Guevara. It is sometimes
thought that one of the reasons why young Latin Americans do not offer themselves for ordination is that the
image of the priesthood lacks masculinity — that religion is
something for women. If that is so, at least Camilo Torres
has put *machismo* back into Christianity. Other Marxist
clergy have been rather more economical with their lives.
The most organized were the 450 who gathered at Santiago in 1972 — while Allende was President of Chile — and
founded the 'Christians for Socialism' movement. Their
object — in the words used in one of the later publications — was 'the rise of a Christianity with a proletarian
character capable of being freed from the dominant bourgeois ideology.'[30] Since the gathering was itself almost
exclusively bourgeois in composition — as is inevitably the
way with South American Marxist Christians — the task
was clearly a formidable one. There was to be 'participation in the struggle which opposes the exploiting class', as
they said in their declaration.[31] Individual Marxist priests
have also been active within many of the official Church
agencies. The Latin American Institute for Doctrine and
Social Studies (ILADES), opened in 1966 under episcopal
authority, rapidly advanced to a rigorous Marxism under
the inspiration of Fr. Gonzalo Arroyo[32] — a Chilean
Jesuit who later campaigned for Allende.[33] Similarly, a
Protestant agency called Church and Society in Latin
America (ISAL), started in 1960 in Peru, adopted Marxism
in 1968 and aimed henceforth at what it described as 'the

mobilization of the people.'[34] Marxist influence has also been evident in religious journalism. The Jesuit magazine *Mensaje,* published in Chile, is perhaps the most well-known. In the later 1960's it attacked Frei and Christian Democracy, for their moderation, and supported Che Guevara and the student political left. Even after the coup in Chile, it has continued to raise a critical voice against the suppression of Marxism.[35]

The high-water mark of the official, respectable progressivism of the Catholic Church was reached in 1968, at the Second General Conference of Latin American bishops, held at Medellín in Colombia. Pope Paul, in Bogotá for the Eucharistic Congress, opened the Conference himself. The preparatory papers, which were the most radical documents ever produced by the Catholic hierarchy of Latin America, were drawn up by the Brazilian bishops under the guidance of French and Dutch priests.[36] Using distinctly revolutionary rather than reformist language,[37] and luxuriant in Marxist rhetoric, they condemned the 'imperialism' of multinational corporations and the 'institutionalized violence' of capitalist society. Intended as an answer to what Mgr. Eduardo Pironio has called 'the profound and legitimate aspirations of the Latin American peoples'[38], the bishops affirmed their belief that radical change had to come by political means.[39] The Church, they said, had to show its solidarity with the poor and marginated – and must do this concretely by 'criticism of injustice and oppression.'[40] Since 1968, many bishops have gradually withdrawn from the advanced positions taken up at Medellín. It is now to be seen in the context of 1968: the year of the Paris student riots, the anti-Vietnam demonstrations, of the pervasive, and heady radicalism of the bourgeois intelligentsia of the western world. The uneasy balance between those loyal to the Medellín outlook, and those seeking to moderate the politicization of the

Church, became evident during the preparations for the third conference of Latin-American bishops, due to be held at Puebla, Mexico, in October 1978. Compromise documents had to be drafted at the last minute in order to avoid a major disruption. As it happened, the conference had to be postponed because of the death of Pope John Paul I. But divisions had clearly become very serious.

Now between the radicalism of the South American bishops and the Marxist activist priests there lies the academic expression of *Socialcristianismo* — though I must use the word 'academic' with caution, because the exponents of the Theology of Liberation argue that their ideas are decidedly *not* academic. They believe they are derived, unlike traditional theology, from social reality. 'We, then, in Latin America', as Juan Luis Segundo has said, 'began to think about liberation before thinking about a theology of liberation.[41] The influence, as Gustavo Gutiérrez has written, was 'to a large extent due to Marx'.[42] The content of the new theology does not come from received spiritual knowledge but from the Marxian concept of *praxis:*[43] of the involvement of the oppressed in the historical process of change. The theologian will be engaged — another quotation from Gutiérrez -- 'where nations, social classes, people struggle to free themselves from domination and oppression.'[44] The Church must be involved in making people aware of the 'institutionalized violence' of bourgeois society, for this justifies the use of revolutionary violence for political change.[45] Salvation is not some 'other-worldly' condition: it is the practical construction of social justice in the existing world.[46] The biblical exegesis of the Liberation theologians is in fact very conservative. With the exception of the Protestant writers, like Ruben Alves, the Brazilian scholar, they have not proclaimed the 'death of God', or questioned the divinity of Christ, as western theologians have done in recent years. It is just that they believe the scriptural texts contain a political message. Christ himself is understood as a political liberator,[47] the *Subversivo de Nazaret* — a sort of urban guerrilla.[48] As Maurice Clavel has remarked, 'Christ has been converted into the John the Baptist of Marx.'[49] Not surprisingly, perhaps, President Molina of El Salvador has publicly described the Theology of Liberation as 'the ideology of the subversives.'[50] The Liberation theologians would be quite happy to accept the description.

They all contend for a sort of South American version of 'Eurocommunism' — a socialist order untainted by Soviet authoritarianism and shorn of atheism. As Archbishop Helder Camara has said: 'the great mass of Communists will give to religion their attention and sympathy when they see it resolved never to give cover to absurd injustices committed in the name of the right to property and private enterprise.'[51] This utopianism is, of course, repudiated by orthodox Communists, as incompatible with historical materialism. The collapse of Allende's Chile, which Marxists attribute precisely to his reverence for bourgeois legalism, and his failure to dismantle the bourgeois state structure, seems a clear enough indication that a peculiar brand of Latin American Communism, or a peaceful transition to socialism, are unlikely.[52] Dr. David Owen, the British Foreign Secretary, has made the same point, adding that the Communist leaders in Eastern Europe made similar commitments to pluralist democracy in the later 1940's, none of which were honoured.[53] One of the main political objectives of the Liberation theologians was therefore overtaken by events — in the Chilean coup of 1973. In the less euphoric atmosphere of the middle 1970's, Latin American radical theologians have come to place more emphasis on the spiritual dimensions of human emancipation,[54] and on the value of folk religion, despite its conservatism.[55]

Liberation Theology also stresses the importance of education in generating social awareness among the masses. But it is to be very ideological education — intended to make the workers and peasants conscious of just how oppressed they actually are. The process reminds one of the candidate in the Irish election of 1826 who promised the voters that he would tell them about five hundred grievances 'which they had previously known nothing about.'[56] This education is known as *conscientization,* and its apostle is the Brazilian educationalist, Paulo Freire, who has worked for the World Council of Churches. At its centre is a distinction between education for 'domestication', as Freire calls conventional learning, and education for 'liberation', that the masses might create, not an 'armchair revolution', but a real one.[57] Freire's writings and methods — according to the 'Conscientization Kit', a packet of literature on the subject put out by the World Council of Churches — are 'pregnant with revolutionary intention.' The document continues: 'conscientization is never seen as having strictly educational objectives. It is always seen as enabling people to take political charge of their own history.'[58] The oppressed are to teach *themselves* about their own oppression. Like the slave in *Meno,* the dialogue of Plato, who solves mathematical problems, though ignorant of mathematics, assisted by the directive questioning of Socrates, the workers subjected to conscientization are in fact victims (or beneficiaries) of external suggestion. To put it bluntly: despite the heavy use of technical language to describe conscientization, it is ordinary political indoctrination. As such, it has been employed by radical priests in many parts of South America. Yet it is also ostensibly encouraged by liberal churchmen, anxious to be in with the educational trends. For them it implies no more than a generally progressive attitude to education, and perhaps to the addition of social studies to the curriculum. It is in this manner, surely, that we are to interpret the endorsement of Freire's ideas by the Church of England's Board of Education in 1973, and by the Anglican Consultative Council in the same year.[59]

In some areas, the Liberation theologians have performed a very useful task. In unmasking the bourgeois values and assumptions hidden behind western Church thinking, they have provided a critique of liberalism which Church leaders in the developed countries would do well to take seriously. They have pointed to the social class references implicit in much of the self-conscious reformism of the western churches — as well as in their own. But the lessons are unlikely to be taken to heart. For liberal churchmen have themselves adopted the vocabulary and style of Liberation Theology, and in the process have diluted the strength of its social critique. As Juan Luis Segundo has noticed: 'Everyone mouths the words, only to go on as before.'[60]

Latin America, then, illustrates the politicization of Christianity in a way which is very characteristic of the Church everywhere. To the Church's real and important concern with the conditions in which people live has been added a succession of ideological superstructures whose content has been acquired, not from a distinctively Christian or religious source, or from a particularly Christian understanding of the nature of man and his social state, but from ideas current within the educated classes of the western world in general. There are, of course, some local features about *Socialcristianismo,* but both its inspiration and its politics are familiar enough expressions of western thought. Western Christians who listen in to the Latin American church, in the belief that this is the authentic word of the Third World, hear only the echoes of their own voice.

5 | *Not peace, but a sword*

The present form that the politicization of Christianity is taking in the world is a particularly hazardous one — from the point of view of its survival as a distinct body of supernatural belief with a unique view of the place of mankind in the Creation. The danger arises in some measure because of the collectivist nature of modern politics, from the politicization of *all* values — so that Christianity, in identifying itself with versions of liberal or socialist collectivism will become absorbed within *their* view of the moral purpose of social order. This is a danger heightened by the decline, within the Churches themselves, of confidence in the past modes of religious understanding of man and of the world. The content of contemporary Christianity is becoming progressively secularized. Lacking a supernatural basis to their world-view, furthermore, Church leaders who argue positively for a political dimension to Christianity are also lacking political knowledge. The call for the Church to be associated with the human struggle for a better society is actually made by those with very little understanding either of political theory or of the real dynamics of social structures. They tend to adapt their Christianity to the prevailing political enthusiasms in ways which are strikingly amateur, and upon terms of association which are not their own. Thus churchmen may be found throughout the world vigorously asserting the essential Christianity of political ideas which, to the trained political theorist or the active politician, are either plainly incompatible with religious faith, as formerly understood among men, or are otherwise notable for having been defined by those whose accomplished political structures will leave little room for religion.

The present politicization of Christianity is also very divisive, for it imports the divided moralism of world politics into the operations of faith. The contemporary conflicts between Christians arise not over differences of theological interpretation, but over sharply defined political beliefs. There were, of course, always political and social elements in the classic church divisions of the Christian past — but, again, there are new aspects of the present tendencies which are particularly problematical for the long-term prospects of Christianity. It is the secular intention of so many of the present formulators of political morality that is the chief danger here. Christians have adopted the moralities of secular political ideologies and promote them for what they think of as authentically Christian social ends. They are redefining their own moral identity and their own claim to significance in society, that is to say, in terms of an external context dominated by ideologies which have no other end for man in prospect except as part of the material process.

Throughout western society, the politicization of Christianity has taken the form of adhesion to political liberalism, and through it, to the notion of a secular pluralistic society. This scheme of things is supported because of its supposed justice: that it accepts the existence of genuine differences of view among men and affords protection to freedom of choice within the diversity. Almost every recent Christian statement about social morality has assumed the fundamental Christianity of the liberal society. Yet Christian opinion also insists on the exclusive morality of concepts like democracy and equality. Politics, in consequence, is not seen as a matter of accommodations between legitimate differences of view, or as a calculation to balance interests, or as a convenience for satisfying the need for basic order while leaving moral refinements to the devisings of individuals. It is viewed, on the contrary, as an expression of the Gospel in action. The modern insistence within the Church for establishing what is regarded as a just society has shifted the whole centre of Christianity, so that it is now becoming defined in terms of precise political morality.

The range of opinion actually agreeable to the Christian liberalism of the present time forms quite a narrow band in the total spectrum of human social organization. Liberalism encourages a false sense of wide choice within this band, and this prompts its adherents to suppose themselves to be genuinely open-minded about political and moral choice. Within the band, furthermore, approved differences of view cultivate a specious sense of real division of opinion which itself assists the disintegrating tendencies. It is not surprising that the politicization of contemporary Christianity should therefore have provoked some massive internal divisions. The new heresies are political options made by Christians who have not followed the liberal creed. Modern Christians leaders are all tolerance when it comes to departures from traditional religious doctrine. But they are ferocious when it comes to departures from the canons of liberalism over such issues as, for example, majority rule in Southern Africa. The contemporary equivalent of burning your opponent at the stake is to give aid, as the World Council of Churches does, either actively or by moral support, to those engaged in armed attempts to extinguish their political opponents in the Developing World. Modern Christians are just as intolerant as their predecessors when it comes to values they really hold dear. They have to be; for they do not see liberal politics as a choice from among alternatives, all of which have relative claims to acceptability, but as self-evident moral truth. They, too, are prepared to eliminate those who don't subscribe to their own moral values. But they do it at the safe distance of Africa. 'God', according to Canon Burgess Carr, General Secretary of the All African Conference of Churches, has 'sanctified violence into a redemptive instrument for bringing into being a fuller human life.'[1]

It is, in fact, to the situation in Southern Africa that I want now to turn. For there is the clearest instance of differences of view, in reality derived from exclusive political thinking, being represented as fundamental Christian morality; and where the politicization of Christianity has reaped its sharpest divisions. Thus Donal Lamont, the Catholic Bishop of Umtali, who was expelled from Zimbabwe (Rhodesia) for failing to report the presence of guerrilla fighters to the authorities, remarked that his actions were 'based on moral rather than political criteria.'[2] It is a classic statement of the position I have been trying to describe.

I want to consider the South African situation as a division within Christianity. President Kenneth Kaunda of Zambia, himself a Christian minister, once actually broke down in tears when he considered the South African situation in this perspective — as a division among Christians, some of whom, as he put it, held 'the Bible in one hand and a gun in the other.'[3] There are those who deny that this is a conflict between Christians at all, simply refusing to acknowledge that any who uphold what they consider to be doctrines of racial supremacy can be Christians. The policies of the government of South Africa are condemned by the leading Churches with a moral certainty which leaves no room for relative judgments. But the issues are more helpfully discussed in less exclusive terms, and without the emotive categorization, now frequently made, of South Africa as a fascist or neo-Nazi state.[4] Nor do the moral condemnations by western Christians assist objective assessment — especially by Americans. It may be recalled that the United States applied exactly the same policy of separate reservations to its own native population in the nineteenth century. Americans can afford the luxury of conscience now precisely because the Indians ceased to be a major problem through the joint consequences of economic attrition and actual genocide.

The South African situation is unusual in that much of the world's knowledge of it is derived from Christian agencies. As one group of Christians first applied apartheid, so it is another which first rejected it. The Dutch Reformed Church may still be regarded as the spiritual arm of the Nationalist Party's policy of Separate Development — or, to use the expression now favoured by the South African government, 'Plural Democracy.'[5] 'It is not too much to say', Trevor Huddleston wrote twenty years ago, 'that it gives to apartheid exactly the religious sanction which the Christian Church everywhere else in the world gives to the idea that 'all men are of equal value in the sight of God'.[6] But in that statement, even from so authoritative a source, is an error. For the Dutch Reformed Church does not teach white racial superiority, nor is Separate Development an attempt to institutionalize *racial discrimination*. The policy, in fact, is not static. Its development, it is true, has been according to rather a different scale of evolving social values from twentieth century Europe or America. As Lawrence Schlemmer, of the University of Natal, has put it: 'most Afrikaner intellectuals think primarily in terms of cultural diversity and vertical stratification', and most South African English-speaking thinkers, 'in terms of class diversity and horizontal stratification.'[7] Now the Afrikaner preoccupation with *cultural* diversity, as expressed within the policy of Separate Development, does not mean that black or other ethnic groups are to be considered as inferior, but that they are to be considered as different — with problems of social and family organization unlike the western order developed by the whites since the seventeenth century.[8] Hence the idea of encouraging the black populations in self-government, eventually to be expressed in a scheme of total devolution, with independent homelands — the Bantustans. Dr C.P. Mulder, the South African Minister of Information, has recently pointed out that — in his own words — 'South Africa's domestic policies are unequivocally aiming at the elimination of colour discrimination and at the goals of separate and equal freedoms for the major social divisions of her plural society.'[9]

Now Christian opponents of apartheid will receive that opinion with incredulity — perhaps regarding it as mere window-dressing intended to mollify a hostile world. They will point out that racial discrimination *is* widely practised in South African society, whatever refinements of meaning may reside within the rationalizations put out by the government. In this, they will be partly right and partly wrong. I do not myself believe that the government's intentions are to be disregarded. They have an educative effect upon society. Their object really is a recognition of the equality and integrity of each of the ethnic groups, but in parallel social units. Where critics are correct is in pointing to the attitudes of racial discrimination and race prejudice which do exist widely in South African society. Yet listen to this judgment, from the World Council of Churches: 'Racism has so permeated the churches and the societies in which they are set, that it has become part of the structure of ordinary life.'[10] This is not a description of South Africa, however, but of western and all other societies. Reference to the literature put out by race relations agencies in Britain and North America will confirm the point. And according to the Kenyan Bishop Henry

Okullu, tribal loyalty has taken precedence over religious and other loyalties in post-independence Africa.[11] And what is tribalism, but racial discrimination in a particularly pure form? In this situation, of almost universal racism in some degree or other, South Africa is still singled out because of the apparent institutionalizing of race differences. 'Probably nowhere else in the world', as Fr. Adrian Hastings has put it, 'is there in existence a more thought-out and systematic pattern of human oppression'[12] — an assessment which perhaps, at the very least, does an injustice to the claims of Cambodia or Ethiopia.

At this point I had better make my own position clear. I believe that the South Africans ought a long time ago to have constituted a multi-racial state. But the fact is that they didn't. They have become, instead, locked on a mistaken course and got stuck with it. As the policy of Separate Development has never been static, so at the present time the progressive abolition of so-called 'petty apartheid' — visible race segregation — the reform of the Bantu Education Act, and the proposal to create independent parliaments and executives for the three non-black races,[13] while all advantageous in their way, do not essentially alter the grand design of institutionalizing ethnic differences. In fact, they seem calculated to ossify cultural diversity along racial lines in a way which, with existing educational and economic improvements, would otherwise prove quite ephemeral. And the rapid expansion of the urban black populations diminishes the possibility that the independent black homelands can ever be an effective means of establishing a satisfactory Separate Development. 'What white South Africans have got to realize is that the one thing they fear most is actually the safest,' as the *Rand Daily Mail* commented in April this year, at the time of the Transkei crisis. 'Only when different races associate with each other... will they come to know each other and reach a degree of harmony.'[14] These are very wise observations. The fact remains, however, that South Africa does *not* intend to move towards a multi-racial state structure, however humane and moral her intentions in adjusting the machinery of Separate Development. What we have to ask is whether, in this situation, she deserves the moral outrage that is heaped upon her by world Christianity, and whether the available African alternatives envisaged by Christian opinion are likely to be any more moral.

The truth is, however, that the alternatives rarely are considered critically. Christian opponents of South African policies are so preoccupied by the race question that very little consideration is given to the possible political consequences of bringing about the collapse of the existing structure — which is, after all, a western-style democratic state which allows much greater internal expression of free opinion than most governments in the world.[15]   Other opponents of South Africa are waiting to profit from the undermining of society resulting from the attacks of the Christian liberals. Marxism, already so evidently on the march in Africa, is having the ground prepared for it. Though represented as fundamental Christianity, the Churches' opposition to apartheid is really also a campaign in favour of liberal politics — for majority rule and economic equalitarianism. Though neither of these have exactly figured prominently in the political arrangements and ideas the Christian Churches have either sponsored or tolerated during the past two thousand years, they are now insisted upon as absolutely required by the law of God. In the case of Southern Africa, some Christian groups — like the World Council of Churches, the All Africa Conference of Churches, and the Christian leaders of the armed Liberation movements — are prepared to shed blood for them on a large scale. The opposition of Christian liberals to the policy of Separate Development rests mainly upon the simple moral ground of opposition to what they take to be racial discrimination. Indictment of economic oppression is also frequently made, however. The demand for economic improvement, made by so many groups throughout the world, is incorporated into black African nationalism. Or, as the Reverend Canaan Banana, of the Zimbabwe African National Council, has put it, in his version of the Lord's Prayer, 'Teach us to demand Our share of the gold, Forgive us our docility, As we demand our share of justice.'[16] There is a confusing war of statistics about relative wages, education, housing, health-care, and so on, waged between the anti-apartheid groups and spokesmen for the South African government. In fact, the situation there is not one of oppression but of paternalism. The black urban populations enjoy a higher standard of living in South Africa than anywhere else on the continent. There is an advanced programme of African education,[17] which even opponents of the government, like Bishop Desmond Tutu, General Secretary of the South African Council of Churches, admits has produced, against all their predictions, the confidence and political consciousness of the young blacks of today.[18] Soweto has become an emotional symbol since the riots of 1976, but the truth is that housing and welfare facilities in that city are, for Africa, extremely good, and the disturbances there are to be seen not as the hopeless frustration of the downtrodden but as the symptom of the rising expectations of those whose standards are already well advanced. Urban violence of this sort is common in many industrial states.[19]

The alternative political structure envisaged by most Christian opponents of apartheid, therefore, is a majority rule, multi-racial state. Unhappily, however, that is a very delicate plant and circumstances are not very favourable for its growth. At the present time, only a minority of the member states of the United Nations Organization have democratic régimes with universal adult suffrage and widespread tolerance of political opposition.[20] Nor does a consideration of the existing independent black African states inspire much hope for the Christian liberals' vision. There appears to have been something of a return to the extensive violation of Human Rights which, according to the All Africa Conference of Churches, characterized pre-colonial traditional African society,[21] however much that society may now be romanticized by African national-ists or Afro-American aspirants to a knowledge of their roots. When, in March 1977, the Conference of Churches attacked the silence of the black governments over the murder of Archbishop Luwum in Uganda, a spokesman told the press: 'they cannot speak out because so many of them are also suppressing human rights.'[22] Yet despite their insistence on western-style democracy for Southern Africa, Christian liberals are seemingly quite prepared to look benignly upon the one-party states which now flourish in black Africa. Julius Nyerere's Tanzania — a country with a rigidly enforced socialist collectivization and a single-party constitution — has received the public support of the Catholic Church,[23] of which the president is himself a member, and the lyrical approval of western Protestants.[24] And a seminar of the International Com-mission of Jurists — a body highly critical of South Africa — meeting in Tanzania in 1976, reported favourably on the practice of one-party government in black Africa. Despite the denial of 'the right to form political associ-ations other than that of the ruling party',[25] they found them morally acceptable. Reference to Amnesty Interna-tional's Report for 1977 will show, however, that, in the words used, 'the human rights situation in Tanzania continued to cause great anxiety', with accounts of tor-ture, up to 1,500 political prisoners, and a situation in which the defence counsel of an accused person is the state prosecutor, and in which the only appeal court is a political party council.[26] Such conditions in South Africa would be hawked around the world as further evidence of gross oppression. Chrstian liberals, therefore are rather selective in their concern with political morality. Their preoccupation with racism in South Africa tends to destroy one system with little prospect of establishing a satisfactory alternative. Some, indeed, are themselves guilty of a sort of unconscious racism in their attitudes to the rest of Africa, by implying that the political structures about which they become so passionately exclusive in the western context, are somehow less to be insisted upon when it comes to independent black people.

Not all the Christian opponents of Separate Development in South Africa are working for a multi-racial society. The Black Consciousness movement is associated with the name of its unofficial leader, Steve Biko, whose death in police custody last year caused such disquiet in the West. The movement, which expresses the outlook of a small urban black elite, is closely associated with Black Theology — the South African version of a demand, first made by black militants in the United States, that the Christian Gospel must become a force for black liberation. As such, of course, Black Theology is becoming the African equivalent of the Latin American theology of Liberation — with the same Marxist categorizations, too.[27] It seeks to render the Gospel in terms of exclusive black culture and black power. Surprisingly, in view of its assault upon white liberalism, the Catholic bishops of South Africa have collectively declared their wish to be 'on the side', as they put it, of Black Consciousness, because 'evangelization includes transforming the concrete structures that oppress people.'[28] What do Black Consciousness and Black Theology stand for? First, they reject the concept of racial integration.[29] They want a black state, to be a manifestation of black sovereignty. Multi-racialism is condemned as 'bourgeois' and 'capitalistic' — I quote the words of the Reverend Basil Moore, who, after his expulsion from South African under the Suppression of Communism Act, became Secretary of the Student Christian Movement in England.[30] In this critique of liberalism, the dialogue between white and black Christians merely indicates the replacement of race loyalty by class ideology. I found this sort of rejection of liberalism earlier this year, when I spoke in Johannesburg to Constance Koza, a spokesperson for the South African Council of Churches. She, too, denounced those who engaged in dialogue across the race barriers, and in very passionate terms, as 'hypocrites' who wanted no structural changes but only a false semblance of reconciliation. We in the west, she said, were just the same as the white South Africans, too: our liberal attitudes were simply a reflection of our lack of opportunity to express overt racism.[31] It is not clear how authentically their attitude represents the general measure of opinion in the South African Council of Churches. The Council's politics are certainly progressive,[32] but the prevailing tone is probably liberal. Bishop Tutu, the new General Secretary — and a man of considered judgment — is clearly, in the available categories, liberal rather than black militant. But the trend, at least within the urban black élite, seems to be favouring the views of Black Consciousness. Biko, an Anglican and a contributor to a compenddium of Black Theology, regarded multi-racialism as 'an integration based on exploitative values.'[33] The real influence of Marxism in all this is difficult to determine. Biko himself, questioned about his attitudes to Communism, was equivocal.[34] Yet he named his son after the Communist President Samara Machel of Mozambique.

It has to be remembered than an agency of the World Council of Churches has claimed that 'a thorough analysis of racism in economic and political relations must often employ Marxist concepts.'[35] The extremism of South African black Christian militancy must also be seen in relation to its American counterpart, which is even more liable to slide into black racism. It was, after all, the Professor of Theology at Union Seminary in New York who declared that 'The Kingdom of God is a *black* happening. It is black people saying No to Whitey.'[36] And it was a South African Anglican, Sabelo Ntwasa, who asked: 'Are Whites to be excluded [from the Church] because they are not black, a physical fact about which they can do nothing? The answer must be yes.'[37]

African Christianity is full of vitality, and it is expanding rapidly. There are now 90 million Christians throughout the continent, compared with 40 million in 1960. The African Churches are also notably conservative in tone — both ecclesiastically and politically. It is the westernized leaders who are the most politicized, and who have identified Christianity with African nationalism. And, as in Latin America, it is the clergy from overseas who are the most politically advanced of all, so that what is now thought of as a characteristically African voice of the oppressed is in fact often theirs. They have stamped African Christianity with their own exported liberalism. In the Anglican tradition I am speaking of men like Bishop Huddleston, Bishop Ambrose Reeves, and Bishop Winter. In the Catholic Church agencies like the Justice and Peace Commission of Rhodesia have worked for the politicization of African Catholics, under the leadership of such as Bishop Lamont, its President, and the American Maryknoll Sister, Janice McLaughlin, Publicity Officer for the Commission, deported from the country after admitting support for the 'freedom fighters.'[38] Western Christians like these have often produced programmes for the 'conscientization' of the Africans — to educate them into political awareness. 'Con-

trary to Western myth, the conscience of the guerrilla',
according to a recent independent Quaker report from
Zimbabwe, 'has been formed not by Marxist indoctrination but largely by Christian teaching in mission schools'[39],
a clear testimony to the effects of 'conscientization.' At
Windhoek, in Namibia, Bishop Colin Winter recollects, the
Christian teachers under his direction 'never separated political action from our understanding of the Gospel.'[40]
This is all strikingly similar, again, to the work of overseas priests in Latin America. In South Africa, as in South
America, it is the liberal and radical ideas of western
theology which are being developed — rather than any
genuine experience of the Third World.[41] African Christian leaders complain a great deal about the missionaries
of the past, who sought to Europeanize the peoples to
whom they were sent, and who confused the Gospel with
European culture. But the westernization conveyed within
the present Christian insistence on liberal political ideology is equally remote from African traditions.[42]

Even the movement for the 'indigenization' of African
Christianity — for African liturgy and African church
decoration, and so forth — typically represents the enthusiasm of white progressives,[43] or of those black churchmen
most influenced by western thought, with all its idealism
about ethnic cultures. The luxuriant Independent African
Churches — classical sects[44] — are the least influenced by
contemporary liberal theology, and are also the least interested in politics. Apart from politicized Christianity, it is
Marxism, paradoxically, which is the other great ideological influence making for the assimilation of Africa to western political and social values. The conflict of the two is
less sharply defined than it ought to be in Africa. The
simple truth is that both are largely concerned with material considerations in their attitudes towards political
change in the continent. If anything, indeed, it can be

argued that the Communists have a more coherent doctrinal motivation. Their vision burns with the zeal of those
whose eschatology and certainty of salvation is non-mater-
ial in its appeal. The Churches, unhappily, are so concerned with their social and racial moralizing that they are
tied very closely to a world of material values.

6. | 'The indwelling Christ'

When the political and social ideas used by Christians to-day are identified and analysed, it becomes clear that they are derived from the secular values of the time. This was, of course, always the case. The main difference between the present experience of Christian adaptation, and past ones, is that the culture of the modern world is becoming frankly secular. At first sight it may seem as if this is not universally true: that in the developing world, especially, large deposits of authentic religious experience still survive in enough strength to dilute the secularism which is imported to those countries through liberal capitalist development or Marxist ideology. But in reality the force and pervasiveness of the secularized ideals of the advanced nations is rapidly producing a unified and world-wide set of responses to political and social questions. The traffic in ideas and the speed of communications, combined with the modern inclination to regard political morality as the centre of all morality, is creating a world which is judged by single, universal tests. Thus once men were prepared to consider foreign régimes which they did not find to their taste as the inevitable consequence of alien culture and social organization. It was the way of things. Today, men demand that their own sense of political virtue be actually applied everywhere — and are prepared to countenance forceful methods to bring their ideals into existence. The instinct which once prompted holy warfare — rather than diplomatic accommodation of diversity — is now rampant in a secularized form. It is let loose in crusades for Human Rights, or to secure majority rule, or to extinguish what is judged to be racism or economic exploitation. These are precisely the sorts of attempt at uniform morality around which contemporary Christians are re-defining the very essence of their religion.

To those who question their wisdom in this, Christians will say that the particular ideas they adopt, and claim as modern versions of the teaching of Christ, are in themselves true — whatever the pedigree of the ideas, however much it may be possible to discern their origin in class ideology, cultural accident, or secularized moral enthusiasm. And they may be right in this. The validity of *religious* experience, for example, is not in any way diminished by showing the psychological nuts-and-bolts, or the cultural conditioning, which mould and fashion the form in which it is evident to men's understanding. For our humanity is the conductor of spirituality. That is almost a definition of human life. So the truth of political or social ideals is not denied by explaining the social circumstances or class attributes which may account for their appeal. But the position is radically altered when we turn to Christ's teaching, whose call upon the loyalty of men depends upon its unique authority — as originating outside historical circumstances — and upon its deliberate evocation of timelessness. That should make us cautious in identifying the ultimate purposes of God with the shifting values of contemporary society. And, above all, the highly relative nature of human expectations should make us sceptical, to say the least, of the tendency which now regards religion as by nature centred in social activism; sceptical, that is, of statements from Christian organizations or leaders which elevate political virtue as the test of authentic belief. These, however, are extremely common. Thus one of the commissions of the World Council of Churches has referred to 'the need for theology to be rooted in the day-to-day struggle of the people to overcome the conditions which sentence them to poverty and oppression.'[1] And the official Anglican Consultative Council, in another random example, has described the words of the Virgin, in the *Magnificat*, as praising the Lord for what the Council calls 'radical changes in economic, political, and social structures.'[2]

This is not to deny that biblical teachings have social consequences; they obviously do. But it is to caution against the sort of consequences now conventionally assumed within the Churches. In the examples I have given, the vocabulary used is not merely a contemporary rendition of biblical meaning, as those who employ it like to suppose; in reality, this sort of rhetoric indicates those social ideals as originating pretty firmly in contemporary political ideology. The creditability of the ideals is also short-lived, as the orthodoxies of thought within western liberalism now rise and decline with remarkable rapidity, dragging the perpetual reinterpretation of the content of Christianity along with them. Today's solemn declaration of the 'true' purpose of Christ's teachings is tomorrow's reviled illustration of false 'prophecy'.

Contemporary advocates of Christian political activism, caught up in the moral fervour of their various enterprises, are often unaware of this sort of perspective − of how swiftly the ideals promoted for explicit Christian reasons are superseded by others. They cannot see the wood for the trees. Their enthusiasm is such that they are unhesitatingly convinced of the inherent Christianity of any moral ideal which seems calculated to improve the lot of men. Some others *are* aware of the difficulties, yet are unconvinced that there is anything at fault with the equation of Christianity with the secular moral sense. For these churchmen − among whom are the most prestigious and influential Church thinkers of the day − the value of the secular is made positive. Correctly perceiving that God

speaks through the created order of the material world in
diverse ways, they have come to regard the Christian
Church, rather less correctly, as a critique which operates
within each successive development of human moral idealism. Lacking a distinct sense of the uniqueness of the
Christian revelation, impressed both by Humanism and by
the insights of other religious systems, and convinced that
the abandonment of the cosmology endorsed by the
Church over most of its existence has weakened its claim
to an exclusively religious interpretation of the world,
these Christians now contend that each progression of
human moral awareness, however secular in form and
explanation, in fact conveys authentic religion. And
authentic religion they define around the fulfilment of
human needs. They are unhappy about divisions between
the sacred and the secular, and regard previous understandings of Christianity as having been too preoccupied
with personal spirituality and eternity, and too little concerned with the pursuit of a just society on earth. But
there is a fundamental difficulty in this position. In order
to see Christ's teaching expressed in the secular moral
seriousness of the day it is necessary for these Christians to
presuppose that the Christian faith comprises a clear and
agreed body of religious experience which can be brought
to bear upon contemporary ideals. Yet most of the advocates of Christian social activism are also notable for their
attempts to reconstruct the whole nature of our understanding both of the Christian past and of the person and
claims of Christ himself. And they do this with materials
derived from the very moral enthusiasms of the present
time to which they are seeking to bring an external
'Christian' critique. They do not have another world to
stand upon in order that they may move this one.

Now there may be sound enough reasons for men to
act in the hope of preventing the suffering and lessening

the injustices of human society, and for Christians to
involve themselves in the political consequences. But
there are no sound reasons, in my judgment, for identifying the accompanying political ideals as either in themselves true, or as forming the content or necessary application of Christianity. For human aspirations to a better
or more just social order are about expectations. They
are about what we think life owes us or what we deserve,
and how we would like to see these benefits and responsibilities distributed to others. Expectations, however, are
not ultimately derived from rational calculation, though
men themselves believe that the rationalizations in which
they represent their emotional impulsions are the result
of intellectual decision. Religion is greatly involved here,
because it is crucially concerned with just those emotional
springs of action which prompt human concern about
individual and social claims to significance. Men express
their expectations in the language of rights and principles;
they connect them to higher laws of human development.
Religion, in contrast, points back to the prior emotional
mechanisms. It internalizes the matter of human aspirations and shows how greatly they reflect, not a reasoned
appreciation of moral law, but each man's unreasonable
claim to significance and reward. Religion is centred, that
is to say, on the facts of human nature, and a human
nature properly understood — from a Christian point of
view — as corrupted and partial, so that even in our most
noble attempts at altruism we find ourselves constantly
involved in moral ambiguity and flawed intention.

True religion points to the condition of the inward soul
of man. It is therefore sceptical of the contemporary passion of Christians to reinterpret the faith so that it shall
become a component of the modern world's political idealism. In Christianity, as it was delivered by the saints and
scholars of the centuries, men are first directed to the im-

perfections of their own natures, and not to the ration-alized imperfections of human society. An awareness of social values is actually involved in this however, as a necessary preliminary for comprehension of the condition-ing that spirituality receives as it filters through the screens of human society. This should not lead, as, alas, it now often does, to the Christian espousal of social *principles,* but to an awareness of the relativity of *all* human values. In their pilgrimage through the world, Christians who are wise in their time always return from the fading enthusi-asms of unfulfilled improvements to a more perceptive understanding of the inward nature of spirituality. So Lord Reith, who as a young man spoke with certain conviction about what he called the 'absolute practicability' of Chris-tianity to the world's social and political problems,[3] came eventually, amidst the disappointments and realism of his closing years, to believe that, as he then put it, 'we haven't begun to comprehend the mystery and the magic of the indwelling Christ.'[4]

At the centre of the Christian religion, Christ remains unchanging in a world of perpetual social change and mutating values. To identify him with the passing enthusi-asms of men — each one of which, in its time of accept-ance, seems permanently true — is to lose him amidst the shifting superstructure of human idealism. But the coming of Christ into the world, the Incarnation of God, confirm-ed men's ancient sense that the divinity they had perceived implicit in the nature of things was real enough. God became man: the metaphysical realm of values was made objective in flesh. The crude and the relative inclinations of men towards a knowledge of the Infinite — whose rep-resentations are now examined by anthropologists — were shown to have a real basis. The visible and the unseen world were briefly joined, and the supervening force of the divine flowed down upon the earth. For, in Christ, men's initial knowledge was not confirmed merely; they were also redeemed. The emphasis of contemporary Christian interpretation of the Gospels is to see an activist, Humanist Christ, whose message involved his followers in social transformation. A reading of the Gospels less in-debted to present values, however, will reveal the true Christ of history in the spiritual depiction of a man who directed others to turn away from the preoccupations of human society. At his baptism in the River Jordan, Jesus initiated a ministry that was characterized by a call to personal redemption, to the renunciation of sin, and a departure from the world's values. It was also a rejection of the politicized official religion of his day. Time was short; eternity pressed near. On the hills of Galilee, and among the fishermen and craftsmen of the lakeshore, he spoke of the urgent need for men to give up their wordly concerns, and even, if need be, to leave family and employ-ment for his sake. Some left their nets and followed him. With stark insistence upon the singularity of the life of grace, Jesus called us to a Kingdom which was not of this world; one, nevertheless, which men enter, while still on earth, by being, as he said to Nicodemus — in that most ethereal of images — born again. How far this all seems from the contemporary understanding of Christianity, with its ready endorsement of today's expectations to higher living standards, its consecration of the political moralizing of the secular intelligence, its belief in a real and actual kingdom of righteousness, set up on earth, by armed guerrillas and Marxist intellectuals. 'By virtue of her function and field of action', as the second Vatican Council rightly declared, in contrast, 'the Church is quite distinct from the political community and uncommitted to any political system; she is at once the sign and the guarantee that human personality transcends the field of politics.'[5]

In the world, the Christian seeks to apply the great love of God as well as he can in contemporary terms. And that will actually involve corporate social and political action. But unlike the secular moralizers whom the Christian activists of the present day so closely resemble, the wise aspirant to eternity will recognize no hope of a better social order in his endeavours, for he knows that the expectations of men are incapable of satisfaction. Before even the goal of one generation is achieved, another sets other goals. 'Take therefore no thought for the morrow', Jesus told his disciples, 'for the morrow shall take thought for the things of itself.' Similarly, Christians are unwise to cling to past models of idealized embodiments of religious order. Conservatives fall into the same error as the progressives, whose politicized Christianity they dislike for political reasons, if they seek to protect a social order of their own preference, of the present or of the past.

Christians are those who act under the permanent rule that the ways of God are not the ways of men. They will cooperate with others to promote the eradication of agreed injustices, but they will, unlike them, recognize that their language of principles, and the cultural materials in which they are expressed, are wholly unstable. They will act, therefore, as individuals, not merely in charitable palliatives but in corporate and political action, according to their understanding. They are men with a knowledge of imperfection, and their pursuit of the service of others is not in the false supposition that religious truth is realized in the process. There can be no proper identification of Christianity with human idealism. Cooperation with the world is always on the world's own terms. And today, that means an agreed morality. But morality is not the essence of Christianity — which is about the evocation of the unearthly. Within Christianity, morality is the structure of behaviour inherited by Jesus from the Jewish tradition

and confirmed by him; it is the discipline which best en-
ables men to order their lives that they might discern the
shadow of eternity cast over time; it is an education of the
soul. Moral behaviour — or love of neighbour, as Christians
call it — is an essential sign of the operation of faith. But
it is not itself Christianity, and in the Gospels the teachings
of the Saviour clearly describes a personal rather than a
social morality. How different, again, this is from so much
that is assumed within contemporary Christianity, with its
theologians' preparedness to reduce what once were the
unique revelations of eternity to a desiccating and secularized blueprint for moral concern, and with its leaders' insistence on the priority of social change over the cultivation
of personal spirituality. And all this, too, because of their
confident acceptance of the moral seriousness of this
generation, a generation notable for its secularization and
instability.

To contend, as I am doing, for the separation of individual Christian action from the corporate witness of the
Church, and to regard Christianity as being by nature concerned primarily with the relationship of the soul to eternity, is these days denounced within Christian opinion as a
'privatization' of religion. I think that is exactly what it is.
For I suppose that only the Christian who has induced his
own soul into a sense of the immanence of the celestial
realities may profitably begin to help his brothers in the
present world. As a matter of fact, the modern politicized Christians also 'privatize' religion. For the faith
that was originally intended for the simple and the sinner
is, by them, converted into an elaborate affair of intellectual judgment and moral calculation. It is made into a
choice of correct social ideals. Now that is profoundly
individualistic: each man no longer has to surrender himself empty before God, as in the received versions of religion. He has now actively to reason and to assent to a

whole scheme of social ideology. As Christianity becomes more like a sect or cult within the pluralism of social values, it also becomes more individualistic and more 'privatized.'

Sometimes Christian leaders see the risk that their religion will be absorbed by alien ideals but wrongly interpret what it means. Here are some words from the report of a consultation held by the World Council of Churches in 1974: 'The Church is always in danger of becoming a handmaiden of dominant groups and powerful societies, thereby losing the possibility of maintaining a critical distance from their cultural and social assumptions. It can only perform its prophetic and critical role if it can avoid being inextricably bound up with dominant culture and ideological patterns.'[6] That is indeed the case. But these words were linked to an identification of Christianity with contemporary Human Rights ideology. The delegates, that is to say, used a correct diagnosis to criticize the association of religion with conservative political values, but only as a prelude to associating it with liberal and progressive ones. The truth is that *all* such values are relative, and a sound interpretation of faith will not allow that it has an embodiment in any political regime or moral ideal. Julius Nyerere's Tanzanian Christian socialism is no more 'Christian' in this sense than Franco's Fascist Spain. Both illustrate honest and passionate beliefs about the institutional expression which Christian teaching may receive. Both examples show a false association of religious truth with political idealism. It is what has always happened. In 1846, Richard Cobden made a speech to celebrate what he called 'the most important event in history since the coming of Christ'.[7] He was referring to the repeal of the Corn Laws. Earlier this year I heard a Church of England clergyman say on the radio that the Sex Pistols songs are 'about world order', and 'changing the world'. This he linked with true

Christian 'prophecy'.[8] Actually, although these examples seem absurd, the investing of nineteenth-century economic liberalism and Punk Rock with Christian authority is precisely what also happens when bishops and theologians endorse social democracy or cultural pluralism.

The truth is that men will believe just about anything that satisfies their sense of righteousness, their claim to personal significance, or their inherent instinct for the divine. Their impulses are constant; it is the circumstances in which they are expressed that change. Thus in the moralists of the present day — the educational theorists, the committed intellectuals, the social workers, and so on — it is possible to recognize the secularized representations of psychological types. A century ago they would all have been clergymen. The ideas they adopt are relative. But to their exponents they appear as permanent truths, as real principles established upon enlightened rationality.

It is an unhappy paradox that the world-view which most approximates to Christ's own sense of the worthlessness of human values is the one which, on being rediscovered in the nineteenth century, led to great loss of faith. For it was historical relativism, much more than scientific inquiry, which appeared to vitiate the authority of biblical and religious tradition. Under the impact of historical criticism the experience of the Jewish people was stripped of its unique attributes. Thereafter men saw, not the special dispensation of God, but only a tribal people formalizing in ritual and taboo the events which accompanied and legitimized their seizure of territory from others. It has been left to the theologians of our own day to move on and depict Jesus himself as a Galilean rabbinical reformer mistaken for God by the excited peoples of a disturbed province. As with so much of the present outlook of Christian thought, however, this realism about the conditioning of knowledge is correct, but the interpretation put upon it is wrong. The circumstances were relative but not the truth which they conveyed. For it was the Incarnation of God in Christ which is the one event in history that stands outside the cultural values of men, though men see it, of course, in the cultural materials of its moment in time and with the cultural expectations of succeeding ages. But knowledge of God, because of the Incarnation, does not depend upon some emotional experience of the individual: it is derived from the inherited and learned traditional knowledge about his presence among men. And redemption is made active in us, not by reliance upon the idealism of men, but in the rejection of the world's priorities, in a recognition of the relativity of men's values. Christians, therefore, see the decisiveness of circumstance in the means by which men invest their emotional demands with ideological superstructures. They see how social, economic and cultural realities mould the expectations of men. But they see, also, the Christ who said he was before Abraham, and who is forever reminding men that heaven and earth shall pass away.

The most urgent task of Christianity in our day is to rediscover that sense of historical relativism, before the faith itself is absorbed by a single historical interpretation. It is to return to the version of history actually recorded in the Scriptures. For there we find, certainly, very particular contexts for the dealings of God with men. But the God who appears is always depicted as objectively separate from the world of human values. He is the Lord of history, whose will is not explained within generalized models of historical causation, but in the retribution and forgiveness which he brings to those who set up the passing standards of human society as if they were the judgments of eternity. It is an account of the rise and fall of kingdoms and peoples: all showing God's disregard of men's sense of the permanence of values.

Historical relativism has some affinities with the Marxist concept of 'historical materialism' — which also depends upon a realistic appraisal of the relationship between social fact and the adoption of ideology. It is a pity that the so-called 'Christian-Marxist dialogue' of the last ten years did not explore this aspect, rather than concern itself with the attempt by progressive Christians to reconstruct the faith with Humanist ideas. For what Christianity has in common with Marxism is not a Humanist doctrine of man but a shared eschatology. Marxism, of course, has secularized that too, just as it has made historical materialism philosophically dependent upon dialectical materialism: a central denial of metaphysical truth which must forever rule out the possibility of a fundamental agreement with Christianity. Marxism has, as many contemporary theologians have, rightly perceived the importance of social mechanics and wrongly identified the nature of the purposes they convey.

What Christians most need in our day, therefore, is to see that the complicated mixture of the Infinite in the structures of time is explicable according to the spiritual interpretations of religious tradition — and does not require them to turn, instead, to the inappropriate explanations of secular culture. Both in daily life and in the worship of the Church, the prevailing emphasis upon the transformation of the material world has robbed men of their bridge to eternity. Around them, as in every age, they hear the clatter of disintegrating structures and the shouts of outraged humanity. But the priest in the sanctuary no longer speaks to them of the evidences of the unseen world, discovered amidst the rubble of this present one. He refers them, instead, to intellectualized interpretations of the wrong social practices and political principles which have, in the view of conventional wisdom, brought suffering to the society of men. Around us, however, the materials of eternity lie thick upon the ground, ambiguous in relation to time, lucid as pointers to celestial realities. For the mysteries of the Kingdom are not the commonplaces of the mere inquirer, but the pearl of great price, which only they possess who dispose of all their other goods.

Notes

LECTURE 1

1. Kenneth Slack, *Nairobi Narrative. The Story of the Fifth Assembly of the World Council of Churches,* London, 1976, p.28.

2. *'Jesus Christ Frees and Unites'. Fifth Assembly of the World Council of Churches, Nairobi, 1975.* Report by the Church of England delegates, G.S.288, London, 1976, p.5.

3. Slack, op.cit., p.29.

4. József Cardinal Mindszenty, *Memoirs,* London, 1975, p.11.

5. *Sunday Telegraph,* 7 August 1977; '55,000 Converts a Day', by John Capon. These figures are based upon the statistics analysed by the Advanced Research and Communications Centre in California. Over 1,000 million people are thought to be Christian, more than a quarter of the world's population.

6. Yalena Modrzhinskaya, *Leninism and the Battle of Ideas,* Moscow, 1972, p.219.

7. *The Guardian,* 17 November 1977, 'Church finds some virtue in closed shop', by Baden Hickman.

8. B.B.C. Radio 4, 26 February 1978; the magazine programme *Sunday* broadcast recorded extracts from the Archbishop's speech.

9. These observations of the 1978 Lambeth Conference depend upon my own notes made during the proceedings at Canterbury. For a very brief summary of the two special Lectures, see *The Report of the Lambeth Conference 1978,* London, 1978, pp. 6–7.

10. Ivan Illich, *Celebration of Awareness. A Call for Institutional Revolution,* London, 1973, p.69.

11. Alain Gheerbrant, *The Rebel Church in Latin America,* London, 1974, p.97.

12. *The British Council of Churches – Spring Assembly, 1978: Report to the General Synod,* G.S.Misc. 80, London, 1978, p.3.

13. Bryan Wilson, *Contemporary Transformations of Religion* (The Riddell Memorial Lectures), London, 1976, p.85.

LECTURE 2

1. *The Times,* 21 January, 1977

2. Shelia Cassidy, *Audacity to Believe,* London, 1977, p.305. Nor, incidentally, were they innocent philanthropists. 'They were pledged to join in the

world-wide struggle against fascism', she writes. 'The majority believed that armed struggle was the only path by which the oppressed of their continent could be freed' (p.308).

3. *To Break the Chains of Oppression. Results of an Ecumenical Study Process on Domination and Dependence,* published by the Commission on the Churches' Participation in Development, World Council of Churches, Geneva, 1975, p.52.

4. *One World,* a monthly magazine of the W.C.C., No. 35. Geneva, April, 1978, p.9.

5. David Johnson, *Uppsala to Nairobi, 1968-1975. Report of the Central Committee to the Fifth Assembly of the World Council of Churches,* New York, 1975, p.21.

6. *The Humanum Studies, 1969-1975. A Collection of Documents,* W.C.C., Geneva, 1975, p.63 (Report by David Jenkins).

7. Johnson, op.cit., p.33.

8. Kenneth Slack, *Nairobi Narrative. The Story of the Fifth Assembly of the World Council of Churches, 1975.* London, 1976, p.5.

9. Darril Hudson, *The World Council of Churches in International Affairs,* London, 1977, p.140.

10. *The Churches in International Affairs. Commission of the Churches on International Affairs of the World Council of Churches. Reports 1970-1973,* Geneva, 1974, p.132.

11. *Daily Telegraph,* 14 April 1976, 'How Marx's Sirens lure the Church', by Edward Norman.

12. In his Foreword to Mervyn Stockwood, *The Cross and the Sickle,* London, 1978, p.x.

13. *Jesus Christ Frees and Unites. Fifth Assembly of the World Council of Churches. Report by the Church of England Delegates,* G.S.285. London, 1976, p.8.

14. Slack, op.cit., p.51.

15. Wendy Tyndale, *Chile under the Military Regime,* London, 1975. The author has written (p.21): 'Comparisons with the Nazis are too obvious to dwell on.' This book, with a Foreword by Lord Ramsey, former Archbishop of Canterbury, was published by the Chile Committee for Human Rights — the body, supposedly non-political, which has the support of the General Synod of the Church of England.

16. Johnson, op.cit., pp.126, 173.

17. *Chile. An Appeal for Urgent Action,* World Council of Churches, Geneva, November 1973, p.1.

18. *Elementos De Reflexion Sobre El Comite De Cooperacion Para La Paz En Chile Y El Caracter De La Continuacion De La Tarea,* Santiago, 1975.

19. In an interview at the headquarters of the W.C.C. in Geneva, 13 December 1977.

20. *The Observer,* 28 September 1974, 'Primate in tourist trap', by Timothy

Ross — a feature article on Archbishop Ramsey's visit to Chile, in which he took the local Anglicans to task for not adopting more critical views of their government. Support for the Junta was expressed by Bishop Pytches, head of the Anglican Church in Chile. He condemned 'the total unconstitutionality and illegality of the Allende régime', and added 'it had to be destroyed to save us from a bloodbath and a dictatorship.'

21. *Chile, A Report by the Board for Social Responsibility*, G.S.Misc. 49, London, 1976, p.1.

22. *Report of Proceedings*, General Synod, vol.7, no.2 (February Group of Sessions), London. 1976, p.485.

23. Ibid., p.492.

24. Circulated in February, 1976, with the magazine *Sensation*. It was an advertisement for Chilean protest songs, recorded by exiled Marxists. 'By buying these records through the Chile Solidarity Campaign', the circular announced, 'you are supporting its work.'

25. *Uppsala Speaks. Section Reports of the Fourth Assembly of the World Council of Churches, Uppsala, 1968*, Geneva, 1968. Report of Section III, 'World Economic and Social Development', p.52.

26. Bernard Smith, *The Fraudulent Gospel. Politics and the World Council of Churches*, Richmond, Surrey, 1977, p.23.

27. *Black Faith and Black Solidarity*, edited by Priscilla Massie, New York, 1973; 'African Liberation Movements', by Irving Davies, p.129 (Papers of the 1971 Dar-es-Salaam consultation on 'The role of the Church as a medium for social change').

28. *Outlook*, published by the Church Missionary Society, September 1972, 'Bridge building'.

29. *Octogesima Adveniens. Apostolic Letter of His Holiness Pope Paul VI (1971)* London (Catholic Truth Society), 1971, p.31. This letter was issued to celebrate the eightieth anniversary of one of the greatest of the social encyclicals, *Rerum Novarum*.

30. H.E. Cardinale, *The Holy See and the International Order*, London, 1976, p.301.

31. Hudson, op.cit., pp.19, 40. Centralization of the administration was carried out under the leadership of Dr Eugene Carson Blake.

32. Elizabeth Adler, *A Small Beginning. An Assessment of the first five years of the Programme to Combat Racism*, W.C.C., Geneva, 1974, p.5. This study was written at the request of the Programme to Combat Racism of the World Council in order to provide an account of its origins and ideals. Its author, an East German academic, delcares that it 'is not written from a strictly objective or neutral point of view, but rather from a position of commitment' (p.2).

33. *Populorum Progressio. Encyclical Letter of His Holiness Paul VI, on Fostering the Development of Peoples (1967)*, London (Catholic Truth Society), 1970, p.17.

34. *Segunda Conferencia General Del Episcopado Latinoamericano, Medellín, Setiembre de 1968. Documentos Finales*, sixth ed., Buenos Aires, 1972, p.133.

35. Ibid., p.36.

36. Ibid., p.27.

37. *Uppsala Speaks*, p.45.

38. Ibid., p.53.

39. Ibid., p.31.

40. *The Lambeth Conference, 1968. Resolutions and Reports*, London, 1968, p.74.

41. Ibid., see also p.81.

42. Johnson, op.cit., p.10. See also *In a World of False Peace. A Report by the Board for Mission and Unity*. G.S. 178, London, 1973, *Problems of Communication between the World Council of Churches and the Church of England*, p.15 ('Shift to the Left?')

43. *The Church in International Affairs*, p.31.

44. *Uppsala Speaks*, Report of Section III, p.53.

45. Ibid., Report of Section II, p.32.

46. *Bangkok Assembly, 1973. Minutes and Report of the Assembly of the Commission on World Mission and Evangelism of the World Council of Churches*, Geneva, 1973, p.2.

47. Johnson, op.cit., p.149; *To Break the Chains of Oppression*, p.80.

48. *To Break the Chains of Oppression*, p.46.

49. Ibid., p.47.

50. Interview with Dwain C. Epps, W.C.C. headquarters, Geneva, 13 December 1977.

51. Slack, op.cit., p.54.

52. *The Churches in International Affairs*, p.175; *Violence, Nonviolence and the Struggle for Social Justice. A Statement Commended by the Central Committee of the World Council of Churches, August, 1973, for study, comment and action*, Geneva, 1973, p.11.

53. Johnson, op.cit., p.173.

54. *The Church in International Affairs*, p.134 (letter of Dr Eugene Carson Blake, April, 1972); Hudson, op.cit., p.291.

55. *The Churches in International Affairs*, Draft on Human Rights by the C.C.I.A., (1971), p.78.

56. Ibid., p.81.

57. *Uppsala Speaks*, p.45; Johnson, op.cit., p.118; Adler, op.cit., p.12.

58. *One World*, No. 25, Geneva, April, 1977, 'Opinion', by Jurgen Hilke, p.2.

59. *Violence, Nonviolence and the Struggle for Social Justice*, p.12; Hudson, op.cit., pp.118, 143.

60. Adler, op.cit., p.16.

61. Slack, op.cit., p.7. Of the real object of supporting armed force through

the use of the grants, Dr. Slack writes: 'let it be said with all emphasis that this is precisely what was intended.'

62. Kenneth Sansbury, *Combating Racism. The British Council of Churches and the WCC Programme to Combat Racism,* London, 1975, p.4. (Bishop Sansbury was until 1973 the General Secretary of the British Council of Churches). Occasionally non-white racism appears to escape censure because it is more effective. Justifying the negligible WCC response to the expulsion of the Ugandan Asians in 1972, Darril Hudson writes, 'If racism is successful and eliminates the presence of the undesired race, then there is little left to pronounce about'. (*The World Council of Churches in International Affairs,* p.140). The discrimination involved in concentrating on white racism, together with the violence involved, led to protests, and a walk-out, by some of the British delegates at Nairobi in 1975 — drawing from Dr Potter, the General Secretary of the ECC, the observation that 'wherever the British have gone in the world they have established a racist system.' Dr Coggan, the Archbishop of Canterbury, agreed that Britain 'had much to repent of over past racist attitudes', although he did also point to some creditable items in the British record (sée Hudson, op.cit., p.285.)

63. Smith, op.cit., p.24.

64. Ibid., pp.27-8.

65. Slack, op.cit. p.16.

LECTURE 3

1. *Human Rights: Our Understanding and Our Responsibilities.* A Report by the Board for Social Responsibility, G.S.324, London 1977, pp. 7–8. The main argument used to support the Christian nature of Human Rights is dependent upon the respect owed to men as creatures made in God's image — p.15. The Lambeth Conference of 1978 resolved that 'the matter of human rights' is of 'capital and universal importance', and the bishops pledged their support 'for those organizations and agencies which have taken positive stands on human rights' even when 'the struggle becomes violent' — *The Report of the Lambeth Conference 1978,* London, 1978; Resolution 3, p.37.

2. Ron O'Grady, 'On Human Rights: Worlds Apart', in *One World,* a monthly magazine of the World Council of Churches, No.30, Geneva, October, 1977, p.8.

3. *Conflict Studies No. 91. The Christian Peace Conference. Human Rights and Religion in the U.S.S.R. by Laszlo Revesz, London, 1978, p.67.* In 1974 the CPC declared: 'The liberal interpretation of human rights is not in accordance with the message of the Bible. We regard an absolute concept of human rights, which does not take the historical development into account, as unacceptable.' The CPC is an international Marxist organization, with its headquarters in Prague. Some more reformist Christian groups in the West, recognizing their own insistence on the priority of social change, have attempted to reconcile individualist and collectivist interpretation of Human Rights: see the Report of the consultation held at St. Polten, Austria, by the Commission of the Churches on International Affairs of the W.C.C. (October 1974), in *Reli-*

gious Freedom. Main Statements by the W.C., 1948–1975, Geneva, 1975, p.70.

4. *Gaudium et Spes. Pastoral Constitution on the Church in the World Today,* London (Catholic Truth Society) 1966, p.41.

5. *Religious Freedom. Main Statements by the W.C.C.,* p.73. Report of Section V of the Fifth Assembly (Nairobi, 1975) on 'Structures of Injustice and Struggles for Liberation — Human Rights.'

6. Glenda de Fonseca, *How to File Complaints of Human Rights Violations,* Geneva, 1975. The book grew out of the earlier celebrations to mark the 25th anniversary of the United Nations' Universal Declaration of Human Rights.

7. Amnesty International, for example, regards itself as a non-political organization. But lapses into political preferences are frequent. In January 1978, the Cambridge group distributed a circular which announced: 'one of the major activities at the moment is the mounting of a campaign aimed specifically at Paraguay, and *timed to coincide with the February elections* to be held in that country.' The clergy were invited 'to organize something like a Paraguayan Human Rights service.'

8. Niall MacDermott, *The Churches and Human Rights,* London, 1976, p.13.

9. *Religious Freedom. Main Statements by the W.C.C.,* p.74.

10. *The Times,* 5 October, 1977.

11. The publications of Keston College — a Christian 'Centre for the Study of Religion and Communism' in Kent — show the same development. Its Director, the Reverend Michael Bordeaux, has explicitly claimed that the issue of religious freedom in the Soviet Union is to be seen in the context of the emergent movement for Human Rights in general. See *Faith on Trial in Russia,* London, 1971, p.21. For the present Human Rights dimension in commentary by Keston College, see *Religious Liberty in the Soviet Union,* edited by Michael Bordeaux, Hans Hebly and Eugen Voss, Chislehurst, 1976, p.54ff.

12. Archimandrite Methodius, in conversation at the headquarters of the Patriarchate of Moscow (20 March 1978), insisted that this literature is unrepresentative of religious opinion in Russia.

13. See, for example, *Radio Liberty Research,* RL 20/78 (23 January 1978), 'The Contents of the Forty-sixth issue of *The Chronicle of Events'* by Julia Wishnevsky. The *Chronicle* is a *samizdat* journal which began publication in 1968.

14. *Radio Liberty Research,* RL 23/78 (23 January 1978), 'The Twenty-Eighth Issue of the Lithuanian *Chronicle',* p.5.

15. *Radio Liberty Research,* RL 14/78 (12 January 1978), *'Dievas ir Tevyne* — A Lithuanian *samizdat* Journal', p.3 (which contains an attack upon Darwinism).

16. Trevor Beeson, *Discretion and Valour. Religious Conditions in Russia and Eastern Europe,* London, 1974, p.41.

17. Bohodan R. Bociurkiw and John W. Strong, *Religion and Atheism in the U.S.S.R. and Eastern Europe,* London 1975, p.58.

18. Ibid., p.85

19. Beeson, op.cit., p.67

20. Gerhard Simon, *Church, State and Opposition in the U.S.S.R.*, London, 1974, p.164; J.A. Hebly, *Protestants in Russia*, Belfast, 1976, p.156.

21. Bociurkiw, op.cit., p.73. See also, Georgi Vins, *Three Generations of Suffering*, London, 1976, Introduction (by Jane Ellis), p.21.

22. N.C. Nielson, *Solzhenitsyn's Religion*, London, 1975, p.13.

23. Hedrick Smith, *The Russians*, London, 1976, p.576.

24. Bociurkiw, op.cit., p.81.

25. Ibid., p.82. An example is the case of Vladimir A. Shelko, leader of the Seventh Day Adventists, who served 23 years in gaol. The members of this Church are usually prosecuted for admitted violations of the law. See *New York Times*, 10 June 1977, 'Sect Leader Tours Soviet as a Fugitive', by Christopher S. Wren (on the case of Rostislav N. Galetsky).

26. As by Michael Bordeaux, see *Patriarch and Prophets. Persecution of the Russian Orthodox Church Today*, London, second ed., 1975, p.341.

27. Hedrick Smith, op.cit., pp.530−1.

28. *Constitution (Fundamental Law) of the Union of Soviet Socialist Republics.* Adopted at the Seventh (Special) Session of the Supreme Soviet of the U.S.S.R., Ninth Convocation, on October 7 1977. Moscow, 1977, p.47.

29. Quoted in an interview published in *One World*, No. 36, Geneva, May 1978, p.22.

30. Bordeaux ed., *Religious Liberty in the Soviet Union*, pp.1,24.

31. For a further list of restrictions, see Bordeaux, *Patriarch and Prophets*, pp.17−20; and see the summary of religious liberties mentioned by the Chairman of the Council for Religious Affairs (Kuroyedov) and quoted in Hebly, op.cit., p.180.

32. For conjectured figures of religious affiliation in the U.S.S.R., see *Church within Socialism. Church and State in East European Socialist Republics*, edited by Erich Weingartner, International Documentation and Communication Centre, Rome, 1976, pp.72−3.

33. On the importance of the liturgy in Orthodoxy, see Vladimir Lossky, *The Mystical Theology of the Eastern Church*, Cambridge 1957, pp.180−1, 189−191: Timothy Ware, *The Orthodox Church*, London, 1975 ed., p.271 − 'The Orthodox approach to religion is fundamentally a liturgical approach.'

34. In 1965 two Orthodox priests, Fathers Eshliman and Yakunin, wrote to the Patriarch (Alexii) complaining that the existing legal provisions 'were used', as they declared, 'as a means of systematic and destructive intervention in ecclesiastical life' (see Beeson, op.cit., p.45. For a full text of their letter, see Bordeaux, *Patriarch and Prophets*, p.194ff). The Patriarch denied the allegations and subsequently removed both priests from their posts.

35. Simon, op.cit., p.91.

36. *Religious Minorities in the Soviet Union*, by Michael Bordeaux, Kathleen

Matchett, and Cornelia Gerstenmaier. Minority Rights Group, Report No.1, London, 3rd ed., 1977, p.6.

37.   Bordeaux, *Patriarch and Prophets*, pp.140, 143.

38.   Moscow Radio (North American service), 21 January 1978 (see *Radio Liberty Research. Current Abstracts*, No.3, 1978, p.9).

39.   Quoted in Bociurkiw, op.cit., p.59.

40.   Frederick Engels, *Anti-Duhring*, second ed., Moscow, 1959, pp.436—7.

41.   *Religion in Communist Lands*, vol.6, No.1, Spring 1978, p.49.

42.   Bociurkiw, op.cit., pp.11, 152—7; Simon, op.cit., p.92. The effectiveness of atheist instruction is hard to judge. There are indications that it suffers from the same problem as Christian education in the west — low teacher motivation and boring presentation of the materials. *Samizdat* literature, on the other hand, emphasizes its effectiveness: see *Radio Liberty Research*, RL 23/78 (23 January, 1978), p.4; and *Current Abstracts*, No. 5, 1978, p.6. Atheist education is also given to the old, on the grounds that it is they who pass on religious belief to the young; see *Current Abstracts* No. 7, 1978, p.2.

43.   Conversation at the central Moscow offices of the State Committee for Television and Radio of the U.S.S.R., 20 March 1978.

44.   For a description of the Museum of Atheism in Leningrad, see Anita and Peter Deyneka, *Christians in the Shadow of the Kremlin*, London, 1974, pp.55—7; *Daily Telegraph*, 27 April 1978.

45.   Peter Hebblethwaite, *The Christian-Marxist Dialogue. Beginnings, Present Status, and Beyond*, London, 1977, p.103.

46.   Roger Garaudy, *The alternative Future. A Vision of Christian Marxism*, London, 1976 ed., p.74: 'Christians have been forced to re-think their faith, and Marxists have been forced to re-think their certainties.'

47.   *Radio Free Europe Research*, 9 May, 1974, 'Christians and Marxists: From Dialogue to 'Historical Compromise', by Charles Andras.

48.   Yalena Modrzhinskaya, *Lenin and the Battle of Ideas*, Moscow, 1972, p.232.

49.   N.S. Timasheff, *Religion in Soviet Russia*, London, 1944, p.13; Jan Milic Lochman, *Encountering Marx. Bonds and Barriers between Christians and Marxists*, Belfast, 1977, p.81. Pointing to 'modernizing' trends within Orthodoxy (not yet a widespread feature but particularly evident in Leningrad due to the influence of the late Metropolitan Nikodim), and to the new theological interpretation of Christianity as 'collective salvation', Nikolai Gordienko, Professor at Leningrad University, has urged the need for even more concentrated atheist teaching of the young. In words which perhaps have a wider application he also remarks: 'In effect, once it has been admitted that dogma and liturgy become obsolete, it becomes clear that religion is the product of definite historical factors. In other words, the process of modernizing religion is an act of self-unmasking' (quoted in *Church Within Socialism*, p.96). This must also give an ambiguous significance to the welcome given by Archbishop Coggan to the 'fresh winds of thought and worship' that he saw in the Russian Church during his visit last year (B.B.C., Radio 4, 'Sunday', 9 October 1977).

50. Andras, op.cit., p.43.

51. Kenneth Slack, *Nairobi Narrative. The Story of the Fifth Assembly of the Fifth Assembly of the World Council of Churches,* London, 1976, pp.75—6. *Religion in Communist Lands,* vol.4, No.4 Winter 1976, p.4, for the text of the reply of the Moscow Patriarchate. For the subsequent consultations by the Secretary General, see *Human Rights. Post-Assembly follow-up.* C.C.I.A. Newsletter, No.4 (Geneva), 1976, p.6.

52. For examples of this belief, see *Religious Liberty in the Soviet Union,* ed. Bordeaux, p.15; *Religious Freedom. Main Statements by the W.C.C.,* p.64.

53. Christel Lane, *Christian Religion in the Soviet Union. A Sociological Study,* London 1978, pp.35, 37.

54. *Religion in Communist Lands,* vol.5, no.3, Autumn 1977, p.185.

55. *Radio Liberty Research. Current Abstracts,* No.7, 1978, p.1 (from an article in the Soviet jouranl *Sputnik*).

56. William C. Fletcher, *Religion and Soviet Foreign Policy, 1945—1970,* London, 1973, pp. 48, 95, 96, 121. See also Michael Bordeaux, *Opium of the People. The Christian Religion in the U.S.S.R.,* second ed., Oxford, 1977, p.227.

57. *Conflict Studies No. 91. The Christian Peace Conference. Human Rights and Religion in the U.S.S.R.,* London, 1978, pp.2—3; Fletcher, op.cit., p.47.

58. Simon, op.cit., p.105; Beeson, op.cit., p.63.

59. Lane, op.cit., p.26; Bordeaux, *Opium of the People,* p.35.

60. *Radio Liberty Research,* RL 23/78, 23 January, 1978, p.1.

61. Lane, op.cit., pp.35—7.

LECTURE 4

1. Reported on B.B.C. Radio 4, 'Sunday', 6 November 1977.

2. Quoted in Frederick C. Turner, *Catholicism and Political Development in Latin America,* University of North Carolina Press, 1971, p. 156.

3. 'The Church in Latin America: A Historical Survey', by Fr. Renate Poblete S.J., in Henry A. Landsberger (ed.), *The Church and Social Change in Latin America,* Notre Dame Press, 1970, p.47.

4. 'The Roman Catholic Church and Social Change in Latin America' by Abbé François Houtart, in Landsberger, op.cit.p.120.

5. See, for example, S. Galilea, *El Evangelico, Mensaje de liberacion,* Santiago de Chile, 1976, p.40.

6. *Segunda Conferencia General Del Episcopado Latinamericano, Medellin, Setiembre de 1968, Documentos Finales,* Ediciones Paulinas, Buenos Aires, 1972, p.192.

7. Juan Rosales, *Los Cristianos, Los Marxistas, y la Revolucion,* Buenos Aires, 1970, p.43.

8. See Joseph Fichter, *Cambio social en Chile: un estudio de actitudes,* Santi-

ago, 1962, and David E. Mutchler, *The Church as a Political Factor in Latin America, with Particular Reference to Colombia and Chile,* New York, 1971.

9. Turner, op.cit., p.46.

10. Paul Gallet, *Freedom to Starve,* London, 1972, p.97.

11. Quoted in Derek Winter, *Hope in Captivity, The Prophetic Church in Latin America,* London, 1977, p.59.

12. See, for example, *Segunda Conferencia General del Episcopado,* p.31, on 'sistema liberal capitalista'; and p.45, on 'monopolios internacionales.'

13. Turner, op.cit., p.150; Jóse Míguez Bonino, *Revolutionary Theology Comes of Age,* London, 1975, p.45.

14. Ian Roxborough, Philip O'Brien, and Jackie Roddick, *Chile: The State and Revolution,* London, 1977, p.75.

15. Assisted by Papal teaching: the influential encyclical *Populorum Progressio* (1967) is widely quoted throughout Latin America as evidence of authority for extensive social change. See especially the critique of capitalism, p.15 of the English edition (Catholic Truth Society, 1970) and of unjust world trade terms, p.28.

16. Jóse Míguez Bonino, *Ama y haz lo que quieras, Una etica para al hombre nuevo,* Buenos Aires, 1973, p.83.

17. *Violence and Fraud in El Salvador,* Latin America Bureau, London, 1977, p.27.

18. Roger Plant, *Guatemala. Unnatural Disaster,* Latin America Bureau, London, 1978, p.33.

19. Bernardino Piñera C., and P. Fernando Montes M., 1977: *La Iglesia en Chile Hoy,* Santiago, 1977, p.27.

20. *Elementos De Reflexion Sobre El Comite De Cooperacion Para La Paz En Chile Y El Caracter De La Continuacion De La Tarea, p.1.* A copy of this paper may be found in the Latin American Archive, Regents Park, London, in a folder marked 'Committee for Peace' in the Chile section.

21. The Cardinal, in his letter of 14 November 1975, to the President, admitted that 'the purity of the service might occasionally have been clouded over by the intervention of elements foreign to its original nature', but saw this as 'a risk inherent to every good work and of which no institution can be infallibly exonerated' (Copy: Latin American Archive).

22. Moscow Radio, 'Escucha Chile', broadcasts on 23 and 24 February, 1976.

23. Council on Hemispheric Affairs (Washington D.C.), Press Release of 9th June 1977: 'Pinochet Campaign Against Catholic Church Revealed.'

24. Florencio Infante Diaz, *Iglesia, Gobierno, Principios,* Santiago, 1975, p.23.

25. See *La Iglesia del Silencio en Chile,* Santiago, 1976 (published by the 'Sociedad Chilena de Defensa de la Tradición, Familia y Propiedad').

26. Winter, op.cit., pp.87–8.

27. Bonino, *Revolutionary Theology*, p.49. See also, J. Lloyd Mecham, *Church and State in Latin America. A History of Politico-Ecclesiastical Relations*, revised ed., University of North Carolina Press, 1966, p.158.

28. Alain Gheerbrant, *The Rebel in Latin America*, London, 1974, p.27.

29. Camilo Torres, *Christanismo y revolución*, second ed., Mexico City, p.1972 p.556.

30. *Christians For Socialism*, published by the World Student Christian Federation, Geneva, 1975, p.4.

31. Fernando Moreno Valencia, *Cristianismo y Marxismo*, Santiago, 1977, p.16; ('Documento Final' of the 'Primer Encuentro Latinamericano de Cristianos por el Socialismo', April 1972). For episcopal criticism of the movement, see *Documentos Del Episcopado, Chile, 1970-1973*, Santiago 1974, p.183, 'Fe Cristiana y Actuación Política' (Aug. 1973).

32. *Theology in the Americas*, ed. Sergio Torres and John Eagleson, Maryknoll, New York, 1976, p.32.

33. Mutchler, op.cit., p.388.

34. Bonino, *Revolutionary Theology*, pp.54–5.

35. *Mensaje*, No. 265, Dec. 1977, p.716; 'Chile: sa Future Democracia.'

36. Mutchler, op.cit., p.101.

37. *Theology in the Americas*, p.23.

38. Eduardo F. Pironio, *En El Espirita de Medellín. Escritas. Pastorales Marplatenses II*, Buenos Aires, 1976, p.52.

39. *Segunda Conferencia General Del Episcopado Latinamericano*, p.35.

40. Ibid., p.190.

41. *Theology in the Americas*, p.280.

42. Gustavo Gutiérrez, *A Theology of Liberation. History, Politics and Salvation*, London, 1974, p.9. This, the most important text of the Liberation theologians, was originally published in Lima, in 1971.

43. Ibid., p.13; *Theology in the Americas*, p.407; Moreno, op.cit., p.24.

44. Gutiérrez, op.cit., p.13.

45. Ibid., p.103.

46. Ibid., p.151.

47. Ibid., p.175.

48. Moreno, op.cit., p.85.

49. Ibid., p.102. See Clavel's *Dieu est Dieu, nom de Dieu!* Paris, 1976.

50. *Violence and Fraud in El Salvador*, London, 1977, p.19.

51. Helder Camara, *Church and Colonialism*, London 1969, p.59 (address in Rome, November, 1965).

52. Roxborough, O'Brien and Roddick, *Chile, the State and Revolution*, p.264.

53. 'Communism, Socialism and Democracy', by David Owen, *NATO Review*, vol. 26, No.1, February 1978, pp.8–9.

54. *Ministry with the Poor. A World Consultation in Latin America.* World Council of Churches, Geneva, 1977, p.19.

55. *Historia Y Mision,* Santiago, 1977, p.10: 'La Religiosidad Popular' by Jorge Medina Estevez.

56. Edward Norman, *A History of Modern Ireland,* Penguin Books, London, 1971, p.18.

57. Paulo Freire, *Pedagogy of the Oppressed,* London, 1972, p.41.

58. *Conscientization Kit.* A Dossier published by the World Council of Churches, May, 1975: 'The Pedagogical Debate', a document of the Institute of Cultural Action, Geneva.

59. *Annual Report of the Board of Education (1972–3),* G.S.152, London, 1973, p.25; 'Education: A Process of Liberation for Social Justice' in *Partners in Mission. Anglican Consultative Council, Second Meeting, Dublin, July, 1973,* London, 1973, p.20.

60. Juan Luis Segundo, *Liberation of Theology,* London, 1977, p.4.

LECTURE 5

1. *The Struggle Continues.* Official Report, Third Assembly, All Africa Conference of Churches (Lusaka, Zambia, May 1974), Nairobi, 1975, p.78.

2. Donal Lamont, *Speech from the Dock,* London, 1977, p.11.

3. *The Struggle Continues,* p.18.

4. See, for example, Potlako K. Leballo, *Twilight Time for Apartheid Colonialism,* published by the United Nations Centre Against Apartheid, New York, 1977, pp.1, 2, 4. Leballo is Acting President of the Pan Africanist Congress of Azania [South Africa]. Bishop Colin Winter has spoken of 'the' jackboot of South African control' in Namibia (*Namibia, the story of a bishop in exile,* London, 1977, p.225). As a matter of blaanced reference, it is instructive to note that Bishop Winter has also criticized what he called 'the monarchy and the sycophants that go with it' and other features of English society — including the Archbishop of Canterbury, for being 'pro-bosses' (*Labour Weekly,* 21 October 1977). His political judgments on the situation in Southern Africa, however, are treated with great respect by leaders of Christian opinion in the western world.

5. There are actually 850,000 black members of the Dutch Reformed Church (*South Africa, Progress in Inter-Group and Race Relations, 1970–1977,* Department of Information, Pretoria, 1977, vol.1, p.8). Of the total black population, 70 per cent are Christians and 30 per cent unspecified in the 1970 census; and of these last, the observation of Archie Mafeje about Langa is pertinent. He found that a substantial portion of the black population 'is irreligious, though socialized in the general Christian culture' ('Religion, Class and Ideology in South Africa', in *Religion and Social Change in Southern Africa,* edited by Michael G. Whisson and Martin West, Cape Town, 1975, p.168).

6. Trevor Huddleston, *Naught for your Comfort,* London, 1956, p.69.

7. *Directions of Change in South African Politics*, edited by Peter Randal, SPRO-CAS publication No. 3, Johannesburg, 1971, p.17.

8. Ernesto Gallina, *Africa Present. A Catholic Survey of facts and figures*, London, 1970, p.75.

9. *Plural Democracies*, published by the Department of Information at the South African Embassy, London, 1977, p.4 (speech of 18 October, 1977).

10. *Racism in Theology and Theology against Racism.* Report of a Consultation organized by the Commission on Faith and Order, and the Programme to Combat Racism. World Council of Churches, Geneva, 1975, p.7.

11. See Henry Okullu, *Church and Politics in East Africa*, Nairobi, 1977. The author is Bishop of Maseno South, in Kenya, and a member of the Central Committee of the World Council of Churches.

12. Adrian Hastings, *Southern Africa and the Christian Conscience.* Justice Paper 3, Catholic Institute for International Relations, London, 1977, p.3.

13. *South Africa's New Constitutional Plan*, published by the South African Department of Information, 1978, p.6.

14. *Rand Daily Mail*, 12 April 1978 (leader article).

15. As in many states, action is occasionally taken to curtail freedom of expression and organization, when they seem to be against the public interest. In the case of South Africa, such action usually provokes world reactions, however. In 1977, when the government banned 18 anti-apartheid organizations, all of which harboured political extremists, there was an outcry in the western press (see *The Times*, 20 October 1977). The circumstances surrounding the death of Steve Biko, the Black Consciousness leader, led the Archbishop of Canterbury to suggest, in the British House of Lords, that the claims of South Africa to respect Human Rights required examination (*The Times*, 27 April 1978).

16. Canaan Banana, *The Gospel according to the Ghetto*, published by the World Council of Churches, Geneva, 1974, p.9.

17. In 1975, 21.7 per cent of the black population of South Africa attended schools, compared with 9.7 per cent in the rest of Africa; *South Africa. Progress in Inter-Group and Race Relations, 1970–1977*, p.32.

18. Desmond Tutu, 'Freedom coming for black and white', *One World*, monthly magazine of the World Council of Churches, No.35, April, 1978. Bishop Tutu was formerly Anglican Bishop of Lesotho.

19. *A 'Ghetto' in South Africa*, Pretoria, 1977 (South African Department of Information), p.15.

20. Anthony de Crespigny and Peter Collins, 'Western Style Democracy impossible in South Africa' in *S.A. Digest*, January 1978.

21. *The Churches and Human Rights in Africa.* A consultation jointly sponsored by the All African Conference of Churches and the Commission of the Churches on International Affairs of the World Council of Churches (Khartoum, February, 1975), Geneva, 1975, p.32.

22. *Daily Telegraph*, 3 March, 1977, 'Church Call for Isolation of Uganda.'

23. Most Revd. Joseph Sipendi, 'Christian Concepts of Socialism and the

Arusha Declaration', in *The Arusha Declaration and Christian Socialism*, Dar es Salaam, 1969, p.30. As with the Latin American bishops who have supported or advocated socialism, Dr Sipendi bases his arguments on the Papal encyclical letters, *Quadragesimo Anno* (p.31), *Rerum Novarum* (p.32) and *Populorum Progressio* p.33.

24. See, for example, quotations from Julius Nyerere in *The Radical Bible*, London, 1976, pp.12, 32. In this book, scriptural texts are printed alongside extracts from the writings of men of vision 'to complement' the meaning of the Bible.

25. *Human Rights in a One Party State. International Seminar on Human Rights, their protection, and the law in a One-Party state. Convened by the International Commission of Jurists*, London, 1978, p.118.

26. *Amnesty International Report, 1977,* London, 1971, pp.104–6.

27. This point was recognized by Dr F.E. O'Brien Geldenhuys, in his address to the South African Council of Churches in 1976. Dr Geldenhuys is Ecumenical Relations Director of the Dutch Reformed Church – the first member of that church to be invited to address the Council for nearly forty years. His appearance prompted a walk-out by some black members, and resulted in a temporary division of the Council into 'black' and 'mixed' caucuses (*Liberation, The Papers and Resolutions of the Eighth National Conference of the South African Council of Churches,* edited by David Thomas, Johannesburg, 1976, pp.31–44, 76).

28. *Southern Africa Catholic Bishops' Statements,* published by the Catholic Institute for International Relations, London, 1977 (Resolution of February, 1977).

29. Basil Moore, 'What is Black Theology' in *Black Theology. The South African Voice,* edited by Basil Moore, London, 1973, p.2.

30. Ibid., p.4.

31. Conversation at the Headquarters of the S.A.C.C., Jorissen Street, Johannesburg, 12 April 1978.

32. *Towards Social Change,* SPRO-CAS Publication No.6, edited by Peter Randall, Johannesburg, 1971, p.85.

33. Steve Biko, 'Black Consciousness and the Quest for a true Humanity', in Moore, op.cit., p.40. On Biko's Anglicanism, see *Terror and Grace. USPG Yearbook, 1977–78,* London, 1978, p.15.

34. Donald Woods, *Biko,* London, 1978, p.98.

35. *Racism in Theology and Theology Against Racism,* Geneva, 1975, p.11.

36. James H. Cone, *A Black Theology of Liberation,* Philadelphia, 1970, p.220.

37. Sebelo Ntwasa, 'The Concept of the Church in Black Theology', in Moore, op.cit., p.117.

38. *The Times,* 14 September 1977; *Church Times,* 28 October, 1977.

39. *Southern Africa News and Views,* Friends Peace and International Relations Committee, London, May–June, 1977.

40. Colin Winter, *Namibia, the story of a bishop in exile,* London, 1977, p.32.

41. E. Bolaji Idowu, *Towards an Indigenous Church,* London, 1965, p.23.

42. Attempts have been made, however — and characteristically often by white men — to show that traditional African culture contained elements similar to contemporary political Christianity. See Aylward Shorter, *African Christian Theology — Adaption or Incarnation?,* London, 1975, pp.29, 34; Geoffrey Parrinder, *Africa's Three Religions,* London, 1969, pp.88, 234.

43. John V. Taylor, *The Primal Vision. Christian Presence Amid African Religion,* London 1963, p.15.

44. Martin West, *Bishops and Prophets in a Black City, African Independent Churches in Soweto,* Cape Town, 1975, pp.6—7.

LECTURE 6

1. *To Break the Chains of Oppression. Results of an Ecumenical Study Process on Domination and Dependence,* published by the Commission on the Churches' Participation in Development, World Council of Churches, Geneva, 1975, p.58.

2. *Partners in Mission,* Anglican Consultative Council Second Meeting, Dublin, 1973. London, 1973, p.17. When, less than twenty years before this, Dr Hewlett Johnson, the 'Red' Dean of Canterbury, had identified the *Magnificat* with socialist ideals, it had caused a scandal in the Church of England: see his book, *Christians and Communism,* London, 1956, p.49.

3. *The Reith Diaries,* edited by Charles Stuart, London, 1975, p.83.

4. Andrew Boyle, *Only the Wind will Listen. Reith of the B.B.C.,* London, 1972, p.18.

5. *Gaudium et Spes. Pastoral Constitution on the Church and the World of Today,* London (Catholic Truth Society), 1966, p.79.

6. *Religious Freedom, Main Statements by the World Council of Churches 1948—1975,* Geneva, 1975, p.72 (Consultation held by the Commission of the Churches on International Affairs, St. Polten, Austria, October, 1974).

7. Donald Read, *Cobden and Bright. A Victorian Political Partnership,* London, 1967, p.65.

8. The Revd. Geoffrey Smith, interviewed in the magazine programme 'Sunday', on B.B.C. Radio 4, 19 February 1978.

Index

Africa: black states of, 66; Christian churches in, 69–70

Albania, atheist state, 38

Aleksii, Metropolitan of Tallinn and Estonia, 41

All Africa Conference of Churches, 60, 64, 66

All-Union Council of Evangelical Christians, USSR, 40

Allende, Salvador, President of Chile, 43, 48

Alves, Ruben, Brazilian scholar, 53

Amnesty International, 22, 66–7, 91

Andras, Charles, 40

Anthony, Metropolitan, 10

Aquinas, St Thomas, 29

Arroyo, Fr Gonzalo, Marxist, 51

atheism: in Albania, 38; in USSR, 38, 39

Banana, Rev. Canaan, of Zimbabwe African National Council, 65

Berlinguer, Enrico, 39

Bibles, question of import of, into USSR, 37

Biko, Steve, of Black Consciousness movement, 67, 68, 98

Black Consciousness movement, South Africa, 67–8

Black Power Organizations, 23, 28

Blake, Dr. E.C., General Secretary of World Council of Churches, 18

British Council of Churches, 12

Brown, Dr McAfee, to Assembly of World Council of Churches, 1

Camara, Helder, Archbishop of Recife, Brazil, 47, 54

capitalism: criticisms of, 7, 20; Fascist rejection of, 47

Carr, Canon Burgess, General Secretary of All African Conference of Churches, 60

Carter, President, and Human Rights movement, 31

Cassidy, Dr Sheila, on Chile, 15

Castro, Fidel, Prime Minister of Cuba, 43

Catholic Church, 23; encyclical *Populorum Progressio*, 24, 95; Second Vatican Council, 32, 45

Chile: Churches and overthrow of Allende government in, 20–2; Human Rights movement in, 49; Marxists and, 54

China, attitudes of some Christians towards, 9, 12

Christ, Incarnation of God in, 77, 83; the indwelling, 77; teaching of, 73, 75, 76–7, 78–9; describes a personal rather than a social morality, 80

Christian democracy, in politicization of Church in South America, 48

Christian Peace Conference (Marxist), 90

Christianity: as bridge to eternity, 80, 84; morality not the essence of, 79; present rate of conversions to, 50; once about human fallibility, now about human capabilities, 14; secularization of content of, 57; shares eschatology with Marxism, 84

Church of England: Board of Education and Consultative Council of, and 'conscientization', 74; General Synod of, and Chile, 22

Church Missionary Society, and Uganda, 23

Church and Society in Latin America
(ISAL), Protestant agency, 51–2
Clavel, Maurice, 54
clergy: from overseas, in South
    Africa, 69, and South America,
    45–7; politicization of, 3
Cobden, Richard, 81
Coggan, F.D., Archbishop of
    Canterbury, 8, 9, 33, 39, 90, 93,
    98
Communism, Christian critique of,
    19; *see also* Marxism
Cone, Prof. J.H., of Union Seminary,
    New York, 69
'conscientization' (education for
    liberation), 55–6, 69–70
corporations, multinational, 16, 52
Council for Religious Affairs, USSR,
    37, 39

democracy, parliamentary: criticism
    of, 20
doctrine, contemporary Christianity
    and, 11
Dru, Alexander, 15
Dutch Reformed Church, South
    Africa, 61, 97

ecumenical, use of word, 17
education: for Africans, in South
    Africa, 65; Archbishop of
    Canterbury on, 8; for liberation
    ('conscientization'), 55–6, 69–
    70; spread of Christian or secular
    morality by, 6
élites; and political change, 15–16;
    westernized, in leadership of
    Churches in Third World, 6
Elliott, Prof. Charles, lectures to
    Lambeth   Conference,   10
Epps, Dwain C., of Commission of
    the Churches on International
    Affairs, 21
Ethiopia, priests of Orthodox Church
    in, 25–6

Fascism, in politicization of Church
    in South America, 44, 47

Frei, Eduardo, Christian Democrat
    President of Chile, 48
Freire, Paulo, Brazilian educational-
    ist, 55, 56
Frenz, Helmut, Lutheran Bishop
    exiled from Chile, 46, 50

'Gallet, Paul', pen-name of French
    priest in Brazil, 46
Geldenhuys, F.E. O'Brien, of Dutch
    Reformed Church, 99
Gordienko, Nikolai, Professor at
    Leningrad University, 93
Guatemala, Church and state in, 49
guerrilla fighters of liberation move-
    ments: Marxist priests with, in
    South America, 50–1; World
    Council of Churches and, 27, 59
Guevara, Che, 52
Gutiérrez, Fr Gustavo, Marxist, 47,
    53

Hastings, Fr Adrian, 63
historical materialism of Marxism,
    philosophically dependent on
    dialectical materialism, 84
historical relativism, 82; affinities of,
    with Marxist historical material-
    ism, 84
Huddleston, Bishop Trevor, 61
human life, as conductor of
    spirituality, 73
human nature: former Christian
    teaching about fallibility of,
    replaced by concern with
    capabilities of, 14; religion
    centred on facts of, as corrupted
    and partial, 76
Human Rights movement: Churches
    and, 26–7, 29–34; in politiciza-
    tion of Church in South America,
    49; and practice of religion in
    USSR, 33, 40; Russian and
    western Christians' views on, 42
Humanist ethics: conflation of
    Christian morality with, 10–11,
    17, 31, 78; Marxists and, 39

Illich, Ivan, 11
indoctrination: of children, 8—9; of
    the oppressed, 55
International Commission of Jurists,
    32, 66
intolerance, modern and medieval,
    59, 72

Kaunda, Kenneth, President of
    Zambia, 60
Kosa, Constance, of South African
    Council of Churches, 68

Lambeth Conferences of Bishops of
    Anglican Communion: (1968),
    24—5; (1978), 9—10, 90
Lamont, Donal, Catholic Bishop of
    Umtali, 60, 69
Latin America, *see* South America
Latin American Bishops, Council of:
    Conferences of, at Medellín,
    Colombia (1968), 24, 52, and
    Puebla, Mexico (1977), 53
Latin American Institute for
    Doctrine and Social Studies, 51
Levitin-Krasnov, 34—5, 38
Liberalism, western bourgeois:
    Human Rights movement seeks
    extension of ideals of, 33;
    Marxism and, 7; politicization of
    Christianity by concepts of, 7—8,
    30, 57—9; rapid rise and decline
    of orthodoxies of thought in, 74;
    transmitted to Third World
    Churches, 16
Louvain, priests trained at, 47

MacDermott, Niall, Secretary-General
    of International Commission of
    Jurists, 32
McLaughlin, Janice, Maryknoll Sister,
    deported from Rhodesia, 69
Manley, Michael, Prime Minister of
    Jamaica, 20
Marxism: in Africa, 64, 70—71;
    and Chile, 54; Church attitude
    to propaganda of, 18—19, 22;
    and Human Rights Movement, 27;
    and Humanist ethics, 39; shares

eschatology with Christianity, 84;
    in South American Church, 47,
    50—3; in Third World, 5, 16; and
    western bourgeois liberalism, 7
material values, Churches and, 71
Mindszenty, Cardinal József, 3—4
Molina, President, of El Salvador, 54
Moore, Rev. Basil, Secretary of
    Student Christian Movement, 68
morality: Christian, 40; conflation of
    Humanist ethics with Christian,
    10—11, 17, 31, 78; education
    and, 6; politicization of, 3;
    secular political, adopted by
    Christians, 58, 72—3, 74—5
Mulder, C.F., South African Minister
    of Information, 62

natural law, Human Rights move-
    ment and concept of, 29—30, 31
Ntwasa, Sabelo, on exclusion of
    whites from the Church, 69
Nyerere, Julius, President of
    Tanzania, 66, 81

Oestreicher, Paul, Chairman of
    Amnesty International, 22
Okullu, Bishop Henry, Kenya, 62—3
Orthodox Church: in Ethiopia,
    25—6; in USSR, 35—8; in World
    Council of Churches, 23, 41
Owen, Dr David, Foreign Secretary,
    19, 54

Paul VI, Pope, 11, 52
Pironio, Mgr Eduardo, 52
politicization of religion, 2—3; by
    concepts of liberalism, 7—8, 30,
    57-9; conservative attacks on
    Church for meddling in politics
    as sign of, 49; provokes internal
    divisions, 59; in South America,
    43—9, 56; as a symptom of decay,
    13; in Third World, 6
politics: Christian leaders not
    equipped for judgment of, 20;
    distinction between involvement
    of religion with, and politicization
    of the Church, 3—4; seen as

'expression of the Gospel in action', 59

Potter, Dr Philip, General Secretary of World Council of Churches, 16, 22–3, 90

'privatization' of religion, 80

Protestant Churches: in South America, 46, 50; in World Council of Churches, 24

racism: non-white, 62–3, 90; World Council of Churches on, 27, 62, 68–9

Reeves, Bishop Ambrose, 69

reform, politicizing effect of agitation for, 10

Reith, Lord, 77

Rhodesia, Justice and Peace Commission of, 69

sacralization, of politics in the past, 4,

Sansbury, Bishop Kenneth, 27–8

Schlemmer, Lawrence, of University of Natal, 61

secular, modern term for what was formerly called pagan, 10

secularization, of institutional Christianity, 11, 13

Segundo, Juan Luis, 53, 56

Silva, Cardinal, Archbishop of Santiago, Chile, 49

Slack, Dr Kenneth, General Secretary of British Council of Churches, 26

slum shanty towns: in black Africa, South Africa, and Chile, World Council of Churches and, 28; round Santiago, Chile, Italian priests working in, 47

socialcristianismo, South America, 53, 56

socialist states, and Human Rights, 30

Solzhenitsyn, Alexander, 34

South Africa: Churches and situation in, 60–1; education and standard of living of black urban populations in, 65; policy of separate development in, 61–2, 63, 64

South African Council of Churches, 68, 99

South America: Conservative military regimes in, claim to be guardians of Christian values, 50; Marxist priests and bishops in, 47, 50–3; politicization of Church in, 47, 56, through Fascist, Christian democratic, and Human Rights stages, 47–9

Tanzania, Churches' approval of single-party collectivist state of, 66

theology: 'black', 13, 67, 68; 'liberation', 13, 54, 55, 56, 67; 'political', 13; World Council of Churches on, 73–4

Third World: Christianity in, 5–6; transmission of western liberal values to, 16

Torres, Fr Camillo, revolutionary, 47, 50–1

tribalism, as racial discrimination, 63

Tutu, Bishop Desmond, General Secretary of South African Council of Churches, 65, 68

United Nations: Declaration on Colonialism (1960), 25; minority of states in, have adult suffrage and toleration of political opposition, 65–6

USA: past policy towards native population of, 61; World Council of Churches and policy of, in Vietnam, 26

USSR: Communist Party of, and Christianity, 38, 39; Human Rights movement and, 33, 40; Orthodox Church in, 35–8, 41

Vietnam, World Council of Churches and USA policy in, 26

violence: 'institutionalized' and revolutionary, 53; as 'a redemptive instrument', 60; urban, in other industrial states as well as South Africa, 65 virtues, Christian: tolerance, flexibility, and compassion proposed as, 8

Ward, Barbara (Lady Jackson), lectures to Lambeth Conference, 10

Wilson, Bryan, 13

Winter, Bishop Colin, 69, 97

World Council of Churches, 15—16, 17, 24; Assemblies of, (Uppsala 1968) 22, 24—5, (Nairobi 1975) 20, 26, 28, (Bangkok 1971) 25; and Chilean Communist refugees, 21; 'conscientization kit' put out by, 55; criticizes association of religion with conservative political values, promotes association with liberal values, 81; and guerrilla liberation fighters, 27, 59; and Human Rights movement, 26, 32; on racism, 27, 62, 68—9; on South Africa, 62, 64; on theology, 73—4

Zablotsky, Nikolai, 35